ADDISON WESLEY

W9-BIZ-629

Math
Makes Sense

8

Practice and Homework Book

Author Team

Catherine Heideman

Antonietta Lenjosek

Jim Mennie

Nirmala Nutakki

David Sufrin

Elizabeth Wood

PEARSON

Education
Canada

Elementary Math Team Leader
Diane Wyman

Publisher
Claire Burnett

Publishing Team
Lesley Haynes
Enid Haley
Winnie Siu
Stephanie Cox
Judy Wilson

Product Manager
Kathleen Crosbie

Design
Word & Image Design Studio Inc.

Typesetting
Computer Composition of Canada Inc.

ISBN 0-321-24233-5

Printed and bound in Canada.

6 -- WC -- 11

Contents

Fractions and Decimals

Data Management

Circles

UNIT 7

Geometry

UNIT 8

Square Roots and Pythagoras

UNIT 9

Integers

About
Math
Makes Sense 8   Practice and Homework Book

Welcome to *Addison Wesley Math Makes Sense 8*. These pages describe how this Practice and Homework Book can support your progress through the year.

Each unit offers the following features.

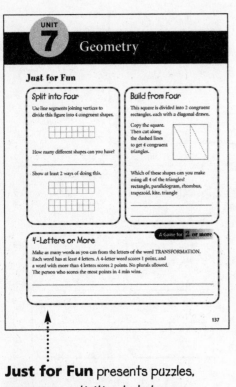

Skills You'll Need matches pages in the *Student Book*. A brief introduction and Examples refresh your skills, and Check questions let you reinforce these prerequisite skills.

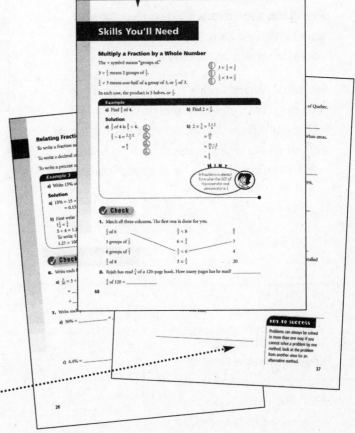

Just for Fun presents puzzles, games, or activities to help you warm up for the content to come. You may work with key words, numeracy skills, or creative and critical thinking skills.

Key to Success highlights ways you can develop your study skills, test-taking skills, and overall independence as a grade 8 student.

For each lesson of the Student Book, the workbook provides 2 to 4 pages of support.

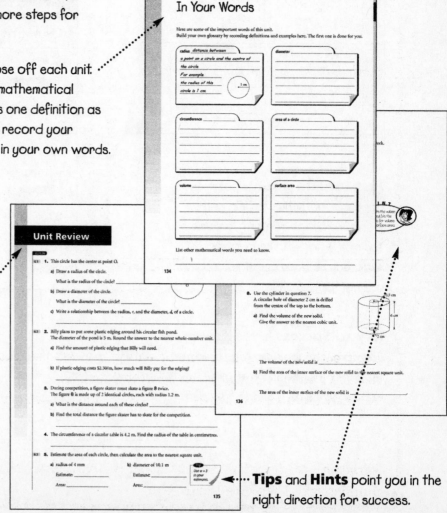

Quick Review covers the core concepts from the lesson. If used for homework, this Quick Review lets you bring just the Practice and Homework Book home.

Practice questions provide a structure for your work, gradually leaving more steps for you to complete on your own.

In Your Words helps to close off each unit. This page identifies essential mathematical vocabulary from the unit, gives one definition as an example, and allows you to record your understanding of other terms in your own words.

Unit Review pages provide the same level of support as lesson Practice. Each Unit Review question is referenced to the relevant lesson where related concepts are developed.

Tips and **Hints** point you in the right direction for success.

Numbers, Variables, and Equations

Just for Fun

Date Palindrome

A number palindrome is a number that reads the same backward as forward. 13631 is a number palindrome.

In this century, February 20, 2002 is a date palindrome when it is written in the day/month/year short form without slashes (DDMMYYYY). Write this date palindrome.

_____

Write two other date palindromes for this century.

_____

_____

Will you have a birthday that is a date palindrome? If so, what is it?

_____

Word Scramble

Unscramble the letters in each row to form a word in mathematics.

ILLTUMPY   _____

BRATTCUS   _____

RAILBAVE   _____

NERPECT   _____

COFTRAIN   _____

LOVES   _____

PENNOTEX   _____

GREENTI   _____

Make up your own scrambled words in mathematics for your friends to unscramble.

Four Fours

Use exactly four 4s and any mathematical symbols you know to make up an expression that has a whole number value between 1 and 20.
You may use symbols such as (), +, −, ×, ÷, and the decimal point. For example: 44 ÷ 44 = 1

_____

Variation: Work with a friend. Make this activity more challenging by trying whole number values between 1 and 100.

Skills You'll Need

Understanding Exponents

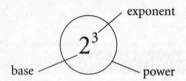

exponent
base
power

2^3 means 2 is multiplied by itself 3 times.
We say 2^3 is a power of 2, or 2 cubed.

2^3	exponent form
$= 2 \times 2 \times 2$	**expanded form**
$= 8$	**standard form**

Example 1

Write 625 as a power of 5.

Solution

Since $5 \times 5 \times 5 \times 5 = 625$,
then $625 = 5^4$

HINT

Multiply 5 by itself until you get 625. Count the number of times 5 is multiplied to find the exponent.

✔ Check

1. Write in exponent form.

   a) $5 \times 5 \times 5$ $\underline{5^3}$

   b) $4 \times 4 \times 4 \times 4$ $\underline{4^4}$

   c) $3 \times 3 \times 3 \times 3 \times 3$ $\underline{3^5}$

2. Write in expanded form and then in standard form.

   a) 3^2 $\underline{3 \times 3 = 9}$

   b) 4^3 $\underline{4 \times 4 \times 4 = 64}$

   c) 10^4 $\underline{10 \times 10 \times 10 \times 10 = 1000}$

   d) 2^7 $\underline{2 \times 2 \times 2 \times 2 \times 2 \times 2 \times 2 = 128}$

3. Write as a power.

   a) 49 as a power of 7 $\underline{7^2}$

   b) 1000 as a power of 10 $\underline{10^3}$

   c) 32 as a power of 2 $\underline{2^5}$

   d) 512 as a power of 8 $\underline{8}$

2

Understanding Powers of 10

Here is a place-value chart showing some powers of 10 in words and in exponent form.

One hundred million	Ten million	One million	One hundred thousand	Ten thousand	One thousand	One hundred	Ten
10^8	10^7	10^6	10^5	10^4	10^3	10^2	10^1

Example 2

a) Write ten thousand in standard form and as a power of 10.

b) Write 100 000 000 in words and as a power of 10.

Solution

a) Use the place-value chart.
Ten thousand is 10 000, which is 10^4.

b) 100 000 000 is one hundred million, which is 10^8.

HINT

The number of zeros after the digit 1 gives the exponent of the power of 10.

✔ Check

4. Write each number in standard form and as a power of 10.

a) one hundred

b) one hundred thousand

_____

_____

c) ten million

d) one hundred billion

_____

_____

5. Write each number in words and as a power of 10.

a) 10 000

b) 1000

_____

_____

c) 10 000 000

d) 10 000 000 000

_____

_____

Solving Equations

You solve an equation by finding the value of the variable that makes the equation true.
You can do this by systematic trial or by inspection.

Example 3

a) Solve by systematic trial. $4x + 3 = 39$

b) Solve by inspection. $50 - 2x = 30$

Solution

a) Choose a possible value for x and substitute in the equation.

Try $x = 5$.	$4(5) + 3 = 23$	too small
Try $x = 10$.	$4(10) + 3 = 43$	too large
Try $x = 9$.	$4(9) + 3 = 39$	correct

b) Since we know that $50 - 20 = 30$, so $2x$ must equal 20.
We know that $2 \times 10 = 20$. So, $x = 10$

 **Check**

6. Match each equation with its solution. One is done for you.

Equation

a) $x + 23 = 50$

b) $3x + 2 = 35$

c) $25 - 3x = 10$

d) $\frac{x}{2} = 22$

e) $50 + 2x = 100$

Solution

i) 5

ii) 27

iii) 44

iv) 25

v) 11

7. Solve each equation.

a) $5x + 3 = 53$ _____

b) $60 - 3x = 30$ _____

c) $\frac{x}{5} = 10$ _____

d) $2 = 2x - 10$ _____

Quick Review

In the media, numbers are often used to present facts, describe situations, compare quantities, and support ideas.

When you solve problems involving these numbers, you can use different methods.

When you work with rounded numbers, an estimated answer is appropriate.

> **Tip**
>
> *When you see the word "approximate" or "about" in a problem, you can estimate the answer.*

When the numbers or steps involved are easy to handle, use mental math.

For more complicated problems, use pencil and paper or a calculator.
Numbers can be exact or estimated.

Practice

1. Use mental math to evaluate.

   a) $6 \times 4 \times 25 = 6 \times ($ _____ $)$ **b)** $99 + 18 =$ _____

   $\qquad\qquad = 6 \times$ _____ $=$ _____

   $\qquad\qquad =$ _____ $=$ _____

   c) $399 - 189 =$ _____ **d)** 50% of $400 =$ _____

   $\qquad\quad =$ _____ $=$ _____

   $\qquad\quad =$ _____ $=$ _____

2. State whether you would need an exact answer or an estimate.

   a) What is your bank account balance? _____

   b) How long did it take you to finish your homework? _____

   c) How many people were at a rock concert? _____

   d) What was your time for a 100-m race? _____

3. The table shows the average number of hours per week spent on watching television by teens in each province in 2003.

Province	TV Hours per Week (h)
Newfoundland and Labrador	14.2
Prince Edward Island	15.2
Nova Scotia	13.1
New Brunswick	16.2
Quebec	13.6
Ontario	17.3
Manitoba	13.6
Saskatchewan	12.9
Alberta	12.7
British Columbia	12.0

a) Which province has teens spending the most time per week watching television?

How many hours is this? _____

b) Which province has teens spending the least time per week watching television?

How many hours is this? _____

c) How many more hours per week does a teen in New Brunswick spend watching

television than a teen in Nova Scotia? _____

4. The U.S. Census Bureau estimates that, in 2005, there were about 240 births and 100 deaths every minute in the world.

Use this information to answer each question.

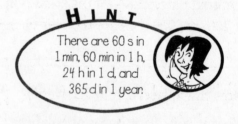

HINT

There are 60 s in 1 min, 60 min in 1 h, 24 h in 1 d, and 365 d in 1 year.

a) How many people are born each second? _____

b) How many people are born each day? _____

c) How many people die each year? _____

d) What is the increase in world population per minute? _____

5. This chart shows the Billboard top 10 albums, as of October, 2005.

This Week	Last Week	Weeks on Chart	Artist and Album	Peak Position
1	-	1	Nickelback, All The Right Reasons	1
2	-	1	Twista, The Day After	2
3	-	1	Sara Evans, Real Fine Place	3
4	1	2	Gretchen Wilson, All Jacked Up	1
5	2	2	Sheryl Crow, Wildflower	2
6	5	6	Kanye West, Late Registration	1
7	-	1	Fiona Apple, Extraordinary Machine	7
8	-	1	Franz Ferdinand, You Could Have It So Much Better	8
9	10	18	The Black Eyed Peas, Monkey Business	2
10	40	10	Faith Hill, Fireflies	1

a) How many artists are new to the chart this week? _____

b) How many artists on the chart have been in position 1? _____

c) Which artist has been on the chart for the longest? _____

d) Which artist has moved up the most since last week? _____

By how many places? _____

6. a) Approximately 3.8 L of oil and 0.5 kg of steel can be recovered from a car tire. If 200 000 000 tires are recycled each year, how much oil can be recovered?

_____

How much steel can be recovered?

_____

b) One tonne of recycled paper saves about 40 trees. How many tonnes of recycled paper could save a forest with 24 000 trees?

_____

Quick Review

A prime number has exactly 2 factors: 1 and itself.

A composite number has more than 2 factors.

Any number, except 1, can be written as the product of 2 or more prime factors.

You can use a factor tree to find all the
prime factors of a composite number.

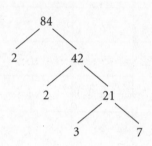

84 is a product of 4 prime factors: $2 \times 2 \times 3 \times 7$

So, the **prime factorization** of 84 is $2 \times 2 \times 3 \times 7$.

A simpler way to write this is: $2^2 \times 3 \times 7$

You can use prime factors to find common factors and common multiples.

Practice

1. Complete the prime factorization of each number.

a) $35 = 5 \times$ __7__

b) $50 = 2 \times 5 \times$ _____

c) $30 = 2 \times$ _____ $\times$ _____

d) $54 = 2 \times 3 \times$ _____ $\times$ _____

2. Write each product as a number in standard form.

a) $2^2 \times 5 \times 7^2 = 2 \times 2 \times 5 \times 7 \times 7 =$ _____

b) $2^4 \times 3^2 =$ _____

c) $7^2 \times 3^3 =$ _____

d) $2^2 \times 3 \times 5^2 =$ _____

e) $3 \times 11^2 =$ _____

f) $5^3 \times 2^2 =$ _____

g) $3^2 \times 5^2 \times 11 =$ _____

3. Write each number as a product of prime factors. Use exponents where possible.

a) $49 =$ _____

b) $40 =$ _____

c) $72 =$ _____

d) $100 =$ _____

e) $108 =$ _____

f) $450 =$ _____

8

4. Find the common factors of each pair of numbers.

    a) 12 and 30

        Write 12 as a product of prime factors. _____

        Write 30 as a product of prime factors. _____

        The common factors are: _____

> **Tip**
> Two common prime factors can multiply to form another common factor of the 2 numbers.

    b) 18 and 27

        The common factors are: _____

5. Find the common factors of each pair of numbers.

    a) 16 and 20   **b)** 22 and 44

    _____   _____

    c) 30 and 50   **d)** 100 and 150

    _____   _____

6. Find the least number that has each pair of numbers as factors.

    a) 10 and 15   **b)** 8 and 28

> **Tip**
> Write each number as a product of prime factors.

    _____   _____

7. Find the first 3 common multiples of each pair of numbers in question 6.

    a) _____   **b)** _____

8. Find the least number with factors 2, 3, and 10.

    The least number is _____.

Quick Review

We can write a number in different ways. Use 23 504 as an example.

In words: 23 504 is twenty-three thousand five hundred four.

In expanded form:

23 504 = 20 000	+ 3000	+ 500	+ 0	+ 4
= 2 × 10 000	+ 3 × 1000	+ 5 × 100	+ 0 × 10^1	+ 4

Using powers of 10:   23 504 = 2 × 10^4 + 3 × 10^3 + 5 × 10^2 + 0 × 10^1 + 4

You can omit 0 × 10^1 and simply write: 23 504 = 2 × 10^4 + 3 × 10^3 + 5 × 10^2 + 4

Large numbers can be written in **scientific notation** using powers of 10.

A number in scientific notation is a product of 2 factors.
One factor is a number greater than or equal to 1, and less than 10.
The other factor is a power of 10.

To write 57 400 in scientific notation:
Move the decimal point to form a number between 1 and 10: 5.74

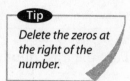

Tip

Delete the zeros at the right of the number.

57 400

Count the number of places the decimal point has moved: 4 places to the left
The exponent of the power of 10 is 4.

So, 57 400 = 5.74 × 10^4

Here are some examples.

Standard Form	Number greater than or equal to 1, and less than 10	Power of 10	Scientific Notation
35 000	3.5	10^4	3.5 × 10^4
5840	5.84	10^3	5.84 × 10^3
60 000 000	6.0	10^7	6.0 × 10^7

Practice

1. Write each number in expanded form using powers of 10.

a) $3560 = 3 \times 10^3 + 5 \times 10^2 + 6 \times 10 + 0$ _____

b) $42\ 621 = 4 \times 10^4 + 2 \times 10^3 + 6 \times 10^2 + 2 \times 10 + 1$ _____

c) $1\ 753\ 147 = 1 \times 10^6 + 7 \times 10^5 + 5 \times 10^4 + 3 \times 10^3 + 1 \times 10^2 + 4 \times 10 + 7$ _____

d) $760\ 018 = 7 \times 10^5 + 6 \times 10^4 + 0 + 0 + 1 \times 10 + 8$ _____

2. Write the expanded form of each number in standard form.

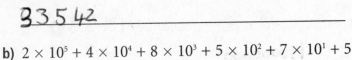

a) $3 \times 10^4 + 3 \times 10^3 + 5 \times 10^2 + 4 \times 10^1 + 2$

33542 _____

b) $2 \times 10^5 + 4 \times 10^4 + 8 \times 10^3 + 5 \times 10^2 + 7 \times 10^1 + 5$

248575 _____

c) $7 \times 10^3 + 5 \times 10^2$

7500 _____

d) $5 \times 10^5 + 7 \times 10^2 + 4 \times 10^1$

500074 _____

e) $7 \times 10^6 + 8 \times 10^3 + 6 \times 10^1$

7008006 _____

> **HINT**
> Watch for omitted powers of 10 for digits in the number that are zeros.

3. Write the exponent for each power of 10.

a) $540\ 000 = 5.4 \times 10^?$ _5_ _____

b) $8\ 000\ 000\ 000 = 8 \times 10^?$ 9 _____

c) $525 = 5.25 \times 10^?$ _2_ _____

d) $32\ 700 = 3.27 \times 10^?$ 4 _____

4. a) One trillion means 1 000 000 000 000. Write this number in scientific notation.

1×10^{12} _____

b) One googol is a number starting with the digit 1 followed by 100 zeros. Write this number in scientific notation.

1×10^2 _____

c) Write one million in scientific notation. 1×10^6 _____

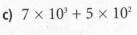
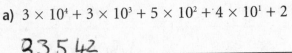
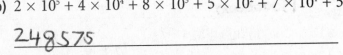

5. The number of hairs on a person's head varies with the natural colour of the hair. A blonde has approximately 1.4×10^5 hairs, a brunette has approximately 1.05×10^5, and a redhead has approximately 9×10^4.

a) Write each of these numbers in standard form.

Blonde: _140000_   Brunette: _105000_   Redhead: _90000_

b) Who has the most hair, a blonde, a brunette, or a redhead? _Blonde._

6. The table shows the approximate distances, in kilometres, of some objects from Earth.

a) Write the missing form of each number to complete the table.

Object	Standard Form	Scientific Notation
Moon	380 400	3.804×10^5
Sun	150000000	1.5×10^8
Pluto (farthest planet)	6 000 000 000	6×10^9
Proxima Centauri (nearest star beyond the Sun)	42000000000000	4.2×10^{13}
3C 273 Quasar	23 625 followed by 19 zeros	2.3625×10^{23}

b) Order the distances from greatest to least using scientific notation.

6×10^9, 4.2×10^{13}, 3.804×10^5, 2.3625×10^{23}, 1.5×10^8

7. Circle the numbers that are not written in scientific notation.

3.4×10^5, 45×10^3, 3×10^6, 120×10^3

Write them in scientific notation. 4.5×10^4, 1.2×10^5

Order the list of numbers from least to greatest.

1.2×10^5, 3×10^6, 3.4×10^5, 4.5×10^4

8. Order these numbers from least to greatest.
26 087, 2.6×10^4, 26 079, 2.6432×10^4, 26 295, 2.6803×10^4

2.6×10^4, 26079, 26087, 26295, 2.6432×10^4, 2.6803×10^4

12

Quick Review

When you evaluate an expression, follow this order of operations:

- Do the operations in brackets.
- Do the exponents.
- Divide and multiply, in order, from left to right.
- Add and subtract, in order, from left to right.

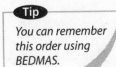

> **Tip**
>
> You can remember this order using BEDMAS.

You can also use the order of operations to evaluate an algebraic expression by substituting a number for the variable.

The height of a rocket with an upward speed of 1000 m/s is expressed as $h = 1000t - 4.9t^2$, where h is the height in metres and t is the time in seconds.

You can find the height of the rocket after 5 s by substituting $t = 5$ in the formula.

$$h = 1000t - 4.9t^2$$

Deal with the exponent first: $= 1000(5) - 4.9(5)^2$

Then multiply: $= 1000 \times 5 - 4.9 \times 25$

Then subtract: $= 5000 - 122.5$

           $= 4877.5$

So, after 5 s, the rocket is at a height of 4877.5 m.

Practice

1. Evaluate.

a) $20 - 6 \times 2 = 20 -$ _____

           $=$ _____

b) $100 \div (10 + 15) = 100 \div$ _____

           $=$ _____

c) $8 - 5 + 2 =$ _____

           $=$ _____

d) $20 \div 5 + 5 =$ _____

           $=$ _____

e) $(2 + 8) - 3 \times 3 =$ _____

           $=$ _____

f) $5 + 3^2 - 4 \div 2 =$ _____

           $=$ _____

2. Evaluate.

   a) $25.4 + 2.7^2 =$ _____

   b) $5.4^2 + 2.8^2 - 1.5 \times 4.2 =$ _____

   c) $16.1 \div (2.5^2 + 1.8) =$ _____

   d) $(11 + 5^2) \div (1 + 0.4 \times 2) =$ _____

3. Evaluate.

   a) $5^2 + 3^2 =$ _____

   b) $(5 + 3)^2 =$ _____

   c) $5^2 - 3^2 =$ _____

   d) $(5 - 3)^2 =$ _____

4. The approximate mass of an ice cube, in grams, is expressed as $0.8s^3$, where s is the length, in centimetres, of an edge of the ice cube. What is the mass of an ice cube with edge length 2 cm?

   The mass of the ice cube is approximately _____.

5. Some countries record temperatures in °F using the Fahrenheit scale. A Fahrenheit temperature can be expressed as $\frac{9}{5}C + 32$, where C is the same temperature in °C on the Celsius scale. Convert each Celsius temperature to a Fahrenheit temperature.

   a) $0°C =$ _____°F

   b) $5°C =$ _____°F

   c) $15°C =$ _____°F

   d) $37°C =$ _____°F

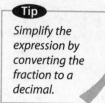

Tip

Simplify the expression by converting the fraction to a decimal.

6. Insert brackets to make each statement true.

   a) $30 \div 5 \times 2 + 5 = 42$ _____

   b) $30 \div 5 \times 2 + 5 = 8$ _____

   c) $30 \div 5 \times 2 + 5 = 2$ _____

Quick Review

A two-pan balance with some known and unknown masses can be used to model an equation.

Adding or removing masses from either pan, while keeping the pans balanced, is a way to solve the equation.

This two-pan balance models the equation $x + 5 = 7 + 4$.

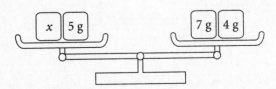

Finding the unknown mass on the balance solves the equation.
To find the unknown mass, x, replace the 7 g in the right pan with 5 g and 2 g.
Now remove 5 g from each pan.

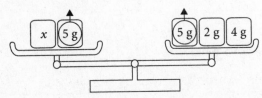

The unknown mass has been isolated in left pan, and 6 g is left in the right pan.

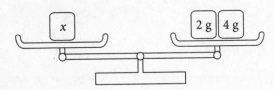

So, the unknown mass is 6 g. That is, the solution to the equation is $x = 6$.

You may solve $x + 5 = 7 + 4$ algebraically:
First add $7 + 4 = 11$ and write $x + 5 = 11$.
To isolate x, use the **inverse operation**.
Since you have 5 added to x, subtract 5 from each side of the equation.
$x + 5 - 5 = 11 - 5$
$\qquad x = 6$

You can verify this answer by substituting $x = 6$ in the original equation and seeing that the left side equals the right side.

1. Write the equation modelled by each two-pan balance. Then solve the equation.

a)
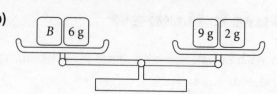

b)

_____

_____

c)
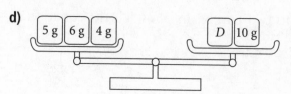

d)

_____

_____

2. Solve each equation by subtracting a number from each side to isolate x.

   a) $x + 5 = 12$ _____

   b) $15 = x + 6$ _____

   c) $19 = 7 + x$ _____

3. Solve each equation by adding a number to each side to isolate x.

   a) $x - 5 = 12$ _____

   b) $15 = x - 6$ _____

   c) $19 = x - 7$ _____

4. Solve each equation.

   a) $x + 8 = 9 + 10$ _____

   b) $x - 6 = 8 + 7$ _____

   c) $6 + 9 = x + 13$ _____

   d) $17 - 8 = x - 11$ _____

5. Verify which equation has the given solution. Circle your answers.

   a) $n = 5$: $n + 10 = 5$ $n - 5 = 10$ $n + 5 = 10$

   b) $n = 13$: $n - 8 = 5$ $n + 5 = 8$ $5 = 8 + n$

   c) $n = 27$: $n + 16 = 11$ $11 = n - 16$ $16 = n + 11$

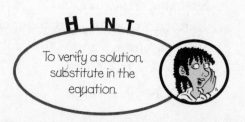

HINT

To verify a solution, substitute in the equation.

Quick Review

As with balanced scales, algebra tiles can be used to model and solve equations.

The +1 tile and −1 tile are called **unit tiles**. The x-tile is a **variable tile**.

One white unit tile and one
black unit tile form a **zero pair**.

To solve the equation $2x - 3 = 1$, use tiles to represent the equation.
What you do to one side of the equation, you also do to the other side.

Isolate the x-tiles by adding 3 white tiles to make zero pairs. Then remove the zero pairs.

Arrange the tiles on each side into 2 equal groups. Compare groups.

One x-tile equals 2 white tiles. So, $x = 2$

Here is the algebraic solution to the same equation:
To isolate $2x$, use the inverse operation.
Since you have 3 subtracted from $2x$, add 3 to each side.

$$2x - 3 + 3 = 1 + 3$$
$$2x = 4$$

Divide each side by 2.

$$x = 2$$

Practice

1. Write the equation modelled by each set of algebra tiles. Then solve the equation.

   a)

   Tip

   To isolate the x-tile, make zero pairs.

   _____

   b)

   _____

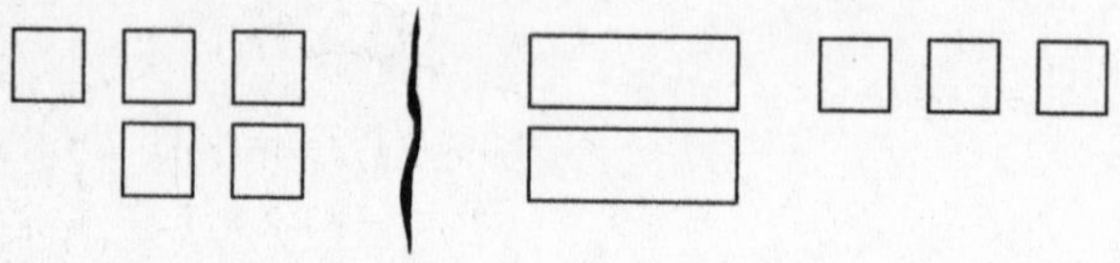

2. Sketch a set of algebra tiles that represents each equation. Then solve the equation.

   a) $x + 3 = 9$ _____

   b) $3 = 2x - 5$ _____

   _____   _____

3. Solve each equation using algebra tiles.

   a) $4x - 3 = 1$ _____

   b) $14 = 5x + 4$ _____

4. Solve each equation algebraically. Verify the solution.

a) $x + 10 = 30$ _____

b) $17 = x - 13$ _____

c) $x - 4 = 12$ _____

d) $13 = x + 9$ _____

5. Solve each equation algebraically. Verify the solution.

a) $3x = 18$ _____

b) $80 = 8x$ _____

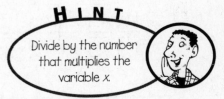

HINT

Divide by the number that multiplies the variable x.

c) $6x = 42$ _____

d) $15 = 5x$ _____

6. Solve each equation algebraically. Verify the solution.

a) $3x + 4 = 19$ _____

b) $5x - 2 = 28$ _____

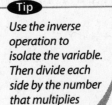

Tip

Use the inverse operation to isolate the variable. Then divide each side by the number that multiplies the variable.

c) $22 = 4x + 6$ _____

d) $16 = 7x - 5$ _____

7. Let x represent each number. Write an equation and solve for the variable.

a) Five less than a number is eight. _____

b) Two more than three times a number is seventeen. _____

In Your Words

Here are some of the important words of this unit.
Build your own glossary by recording definitions and examples here. The first one is done for you.

expanded form *a way of writing numbers that shows the value of each digit*

For example, the expanded form of 3568 is 3000 + 500 + 60 + 8, or

$3568 = 3 \times 10^3 + 5 \times 10^2 + 6 \times 10 + 8$

prime factorization

scientific notation

inverse operation

algebra tiles

zero pair

List other mathematical words you need to know.

Unit Review

1.1 **1.**

The average high school student generates about 2 kg of garbage every day.

a) How much garbage does a high school student generate in a month?

_____

Tip
The average number of days in a month is 30.

b) How much garbage does a high school of 800 students generate in one year?

_____

c) A high school generates 14 000 kg of garbage every week. About how many students are in the high school?

_____

d) Are the answers to the above questions exact answers or estimates?

_____

1.2 **2.** Write the prime factorization of each number. Use exponents where possible.

a) 18 _____   b) 81 _____

c) 88 _____   d) 196 _____

3. Find the common factors of each pair of numbers.

a) 14 and 21   b) 20 and 12   c) 45 and 15

_____   _____   _____

4. Find the least number that has each pair of numbers as factors.

a) 6 and 21   b) 22 and 55

Tip
The least number is the product of the common factors and the remaining factors.

_____   _____

1.3 **5.** Write each number in expanded form.

 a) 2345 _____

 b) 450 _____

 c) 2006 _____

6. Write each number in scientific notation.

 a) 23 900　　　　b) 4 700 000　　　　c) 8 000 000 000　　　d) 200

 _____　　_____　　_____　　_____

1.4 **7.** Evaluate.

 a) $6 \times 10 - 24$ _____　　　　b) $7^2 - 21 \times 2$ _____

 c) $(4 + 3) \times 8 + 1$ _____　　　　d) $(4 + 8) \div (2 + 2)$ _____

8. At a certain range of depths, the temperature of Earth's interior, in degrees Celsius, is expressed as $10d + 20$, where d is the depth in kilometres. Determine the temperature at a depth of 15 km.

_____

1.5 **9.** Solve each equation and verify the solution.

 a) $x + 6 = 13$ _____　　b) $x - 12 = 20 + 5$ _____　　c) $35 - 15 = x + 14$ _____

1.6 **10.** Solve each equation and verify the solution.

 a) $5 + 2x = 25$ _____　　b) $14 = 5x - 6$ _____　　c) $15 = 4x + 7$ _____

11. Five more than three times a number is forty-one. Let x represent the number.

 Write an equation and solve for the variable. _____

Applications of Ratio, Rate, and Percent

Just for Fun

Crossnumber Puzzle

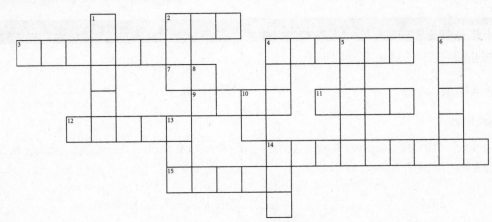

Across

2. Least 3-digit prime
3. 1 million
4. $333 \times 999 + 666$
7. 3^4
9. 60% of 995 + 80% of 995
11. 88×88
12. 202^2
14. $12\,345\,678 \times 9 + 9$
15. Number of seconds in a day

Down

1. Value of 5 in 456 789
2. $3 \times 2 \times 3 \times 2 \times 3$
4. 7^3
5. 189×189
6. 111×111
8. Percent change from 100 to 111
10. Greatest 2-digit prime
13. $(9 + 2 \times 19) \times 10 - 2$
14. 1 as a percent

Build Your Words

A Game for **2 or more**

Make as many words as you can from the letters of the word DECIMAL.
Each 3-letter word scores 1 point, each 4-letter word scores 2 points, and
each word with more than 4 letters scores 4 points.
The person who scores the most points in 3 min wins.

Skills You'll Need

What Is a Ratio?

A ratio is a comparison of two quantities measured in the same unit.

A box contains 3 black balls and 5 yellow balls.
The ratio of black balls to yellow balls is 3:5. 3:5 is a part-to-part ratio.
The ratio of yellow balls to the total number of balls is 5:8. 5:8 is a part-to-whole ratio.

Example 1

Write each ratio in simplest form.

a) 24:42

b) 64:24

Solution

To write a ratio in simplest form, divide the terms by their greatest common factor (GCF).

a)   24:42   Divide each term by 6.
 = (24 ÷ 6):(42 ÷ 6)
 =   4:7

b)   64:24   Divide each term by 8.
 = (64 ÷ 8):(24 ÷ 8)
 =   8:3

Note: The ratios 24:42 and 4:7 are **equivalent**, as are 64:24 and 8:3.

✓ Check

1. Write each ratio in simplest form.

a) 12:28 _____   b) 35:21 _____   c) 30:75 _____

2. Find pairs of equivalent ratios.

4:6	6:9	15:18	10:12
12:8	2:5	6:4	6:15

3. A box contains 8 red, 6 blue, and 4 green cubes.
Write each ratio in simplest form.

a) red to blue _____

b) blue to green _____

c) red to green _____

d) blue to total _____

What Is a Rate?

A rate is a comparison of two quantities measured in different units.

In 40 min, Joey walked 3000 m.
In 1 min, Joey walked: $\frac{3000 \text{ m}}{40} = 75$ m
Joey's walking rate is 75 m/min.
This is a **unit rate** because the distance walked was for 1 unit time (1 min).

Example 2

Ribbon costs $7.20 for 4 m. What is the unit cost of the ribbon?

Solution

The cost of 4 m of ribbon is $7.20.
So, the cost of 1 m of ribbon is: $7.20 ÷ 4 = $1.80
The unit cost of the ribbon is $1.80/m.

Note: The cost of ribbon is a unit rate as it compares a quantity ($1.80)
to 1 unit length (1 m).

✓ Check

4. Write each as a unit rate.

a) 420 heartbeats in 5 min = 420 beats ÷ _____ = _____ beats/min

b) $2.20 for 4 oranges = _____ ÷ _____ = _____

c) 100 m in 60 s = _____ ÷ _____ = _____

5. Roger drove 192 km in 3 h.

a) What was Roger's average speed?

_____

b) At this average speed, how long will it take Roger to drive 352 km?

_____

Relating Fractions, Decimals, and Percents

To write a fraction as a decimal, divide: $\frac{4}{5} = 4 \div 5 = 0.8$

To write a decimal as a percent, multiply by 100%: $0.8 \times 100\% = 80\%$

To write a percent as a decimal, divide 80 by 100: $80 \div 100 = 0.8$

Example 3

a) Write 15% as a decimal.

b) Write $1\frac{1}{4}$ as a decimal and as a percent.

Solution

a) $15\% = 15 \div 100$
$= 0.15$

HINT

One percent is 1 out of 100. 100% is one whole.

b) First write $1\frac{1}{4}$ as an improper fraction.
$1\frac{1}{4} = \frac{5}{4}$
$5 \div 4 = 1.25$
To write 1.25 as a percent, multiply by 100%.
$1.25 \times 100\% = 125\%$

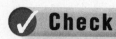 **Check**

6. Write each fraction as a decimal and a percent.

a) $\frac{3}{50} = 3 \div$ _____

= _____

= _____%

b) $\frac{7}{25} =$ _____

= _____

= _____%

c) $\frac{6}{5} =$ _____

= _____

= _____%

7. Write each percent as a decimal and as a fraction.

a) $36\% =$ _____ = _____

b) $0.05\% =$ _____ = _____

c) $4.4\% =$ _____ = _____

d) $160\% =$ _____ = _____

Quick Review

You can often solve a problem involving ratios by setting up a proportion.
A **proportion** is a statement that two ratios are equal.

In a box of red and blue marbles, the ratio of red marbles to blue marbles is 3:4.
If there are 48 blue marbles, you can find the number of red marbles using a proportion.

Let r represent the number of red marbles.

Then, $\quad\quad\quad\quad r{:}48 = 3{:}4$

In fraction form, $\frac{r}{48} = \frac{3}{4}$

To find the value of r, first isolate r by multiplying each side of the proportion by 48.

$$48 \times \frac{r}{48} = 48 \times \frac{3}{4}$$
$$r = \frac{144}{4}$$
$$= 36$$

There are 36 red marbles.

Practice

1. State the number you would multiply each side of the proportion by to isolate the variable.

a) $\frac{r}{6} = \frac{5}{6}$ _____

b) $\frac{t}{15} = \frac{2}{5}$ _____

c) $\frac{v}{3} = \frac{5}{6}$ _____

2. Find each missing term.

a) $\quad\quad\quad p{:}4 = 9{:}12$

$\quad\quad\quad\quad \frac{p}{4} =$ _____

_____ $\times \frac{p}{4} =$ _____

$\quad\quad\quad\quad p =$ _____

HINT

Write each ratio in fraction form.

b) $c{:}12 = 5{:}6$ _____

c) $3{:}14 = t{:}70$ _____

3. Find each missing term.

a) $\frac{f}{10} = \frac{4}{5}$ _____

b) $\frac{h}{8} = \frac{12}{3}$ _____

c) $\frac{w}{11} = \frac{6}{33}$ _____

d) $x:6 = 12:9$ _____

e) $m:4 = 9:6$ _____

f) $x:16 = 5:4$ _____

4. In a bag of coloured cubes, the ratio of pink cubes to purple cubes is 5:7.
If there are 70 pink cubes, how many purple cubes are there?

Let p represent the number of purple cubes. Write a proportion:

p: _____ = _____ : _____

> **Tip**
> Writing the variable as the first term in the ratio makes it easier to solve the proportion.

There are _____ purple cubes.

5. Rectangles ABCD and PQRS have the same length-to-width ratio.
Calculate the length of rectangle PQRS.

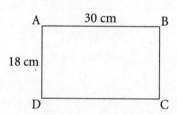 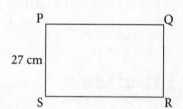

The length of rectangle PQRS is _____.

6. An ad stated that 7 out of 10 teenagers ate cereal for breakfast.
Suppose 140 teenagers were interviewed. How many did not eat cereal for breakfast?

_____ teenagers did not eat cereal for breakfast.

7. On a school trip, the ratio of teachers to students is 2:21. The ratio of boys to girls is 4:3.

If there are 18 girls on the trip, how many boys are there? _____

How many teachers? _____

Quick Review

A scale drawing of a diagram or an object can be an enlargement or reduction of the diagram or object. The first term of the scale is greater than the second term for an enlargement and the reverse is true for a reduction.

To make a scale drawing of a painting with dimensions 99 cm by 69 cm on a sheet of paper measuring 27 cm by 18 cm, you need to choose an appropriate scale.

First find the ratios of the corresponding dimensions.
Length of paper:length of painting = 27:99
$$= 1:3.\overline{6}$$
The painting is more than 3 times as long as the paper. A possible scale would be 1:4.
Width of paper:width of painting = 18:69
$$= 1: 3.8\overline{3}$$
The painting is almost 4 times as wide as the paper. A possible scale would be 1:4.

So, you may use a scale of 1:4, or 1 cm on the drawing represents 4 cm on the painting.

The scale drawing will have these dimensions:
$\frac{99 \text{ cm}}{4}$ by $\frac{69 \text{ cm}}{4}$, or 24.75 cm by 17.25 cm.

Practice

1. A rectangular painting has dimensions 300 cm by 230 cm.

   a) A scale drawing of the painting will be made on a sheet of paper that measures 32 cm by 24 cm. Find an appropriate scale for the drawing.

   Length of paper:length of painting = _____ cm:_____ cm = 1:_____

   Width of paper:width of painting = _____ cm:_____ cm = 1: _____

   An appropriate scale would be 1:_____.

   b) On the scale drawing, a tree is 3.2 cm tall. Find the height of the tree on the painting.

   1 cm on the drawing represents _____ cm on the painting.

   3.2 cm represents 3.2 × _____ cm = _____ cm

   The height of the tree is _____ cm on the painting.

2. The length of a bug is 6.4 cm in a drawing. The drawing was made using a scale of 4:1. What is the actual length of the bug?

Let the actual length of the bug be l cm.

Length of bug:length of drawing = 1:4

$$\frac{l}{6.4} = \underline{\hspace{4cm}}$$

$$\underline{\hspace{3cm}} \times \frac{l}{6.4} = \underline{\hspace{4cm}}$$

$$l = \underline{\hspace{3cm}}$$

The actual length of the bug is _____ cm.

3. The scale on a map of Ontario is 1:5 000 000. The map distance between Thunder Bay and Ottawa is 30 cm. What is the actual distance from Thunder Bay to Ottawa?

The actual distance is _____.

4. The scale on a map of Canada is 1:8 000 000. The distance from Prince George, B.C., to Fredericton, N.B. is 5320 km. What is the distance between these 2 places on the map?

The distance between the 2 places on the map is _____.

5. A blueprint for a mansion has a scale of 1:40.
Calculate the dimensions of each room on the blueprint.

a) 6.8 m by 4.4 m

b) 12.2 m by 7.4 m

_____   _____

6. A new passenger aircraft has a length of 58.8 m and a wingspan of 61.2 m. A scale model of the plane is 39.2 cm long.

a) What is the scale of the model? _____

Tip

Measurements must be in the same unit. Change metres to centimetres.

b) What is the wingspan of the model? _____

Quick Review

To compare different rates, you need to calculate their unit rates.

A case of 12 cartons of juice costs $11.76.
A packet of 3 cartons of the same juice costs $2.88.
To find which juice is the better buy, you compare the unit costs of the 2 packages.
The unit cost of the case of 12 cartons is: $11.76 ÷ 12 = $0.98
The unit cost of the packet of 3 cartons is: $2.88 ÷ 3 = $0.96
So, the packet of 3 cartons is the better buy.

The unit cost can be written as a unit rate:
The unit rate of the better-buy juice is $0.96/carton.

To find the unit rate of a 450-g packet of cereal that costs $3.96,
you may use the cost of 100 g as the unit cost.
The cost of 100 g of the 450-g packet is: $\frac{\$3.96}{450} \times 100 = \$0.88$
So, the unit rate of the 450-g packet of cereal is $0.88/100 g.

Practice

1. Write a unit rate for each.

   a) 6 bottles of juice for $3.96

      $\frac{\$3.96}{\quad\quad}$ = _____

   b) 840 words typed in 12 min

      _____

   c) $564 earned in 4 weeks

      _____

   d) 130 mL toothpaste for $1.69

      _____

   > **Tip**
   > A unit rate could be a rate for a quantity greater than 1.

2. Which is the better buy? Explain.

   a) 475 g of cereal for $3.80 or 750 g for $6.30

      _____

   b) 385 mL of shampoo for $5.39 or 400 mL for $5.72

      _____

3. Find the average speed of each.

a) 242 km in 4 h   **b)** 372 km in 6 h   **c)** 309 km in 5 h

_____   _____   _____

Which is the greatest average speed? _____

4. Shamar types 279 words in 4.5 min, Tasha types 320 words in 5 min, and Cody types 341 words in 5.5 min. Who has the greatest average typing speed?

_____ has the greatest typing speed.

5. In the first 6 games of the basketball season, Lucinda scored 87 points.

a) What was her average number of points scored per game? _____

b) At this rate, how many points will Lucinda score in 26 games? _____

6. Which is the better buy?
Twelve 710-mL bottles of water for $6.60 or twenty-four 500-mL bottles for $9.18

_____

7. Population density is described as the average number of people per square kilometre. The population density of Canada is approximately 3.5 persons/km². Use the data in the table. Name a province or territory that has:

a) A population density closest to that of Canada _____

b) A population density about half of that of Canada _____

c) A population density about 4 times that of Canada _____

d) A population density about 300 times that of Nunavut _____

Province/Territory	Population	Area (km²)
Ontario	12 393 000	917 700
Saskatchewan	995 000	591 700
British Columbia	4 196 000	925 200
Nunavut	29 600	1 939 000

Quick Review

To calculate a percent of a quantity, first write the percent as a decimal.
Then calculate the decimal value of the quantity.

To find 140% of $850, write 140% as a decimal.
$140\% = \frac{140}{100} = 1.40$
Then, 140% of $\$850 = 1.40 \times \$850$
$= \$1190$
This answer can be illustrated on a number line.

```
    0              $850    $1190
    ├───────────────┼───────┤
   0%             100%    140%
```

Percents that are less than 1% can also be illustrated on a number line.
$1\% = \frac{1}{100} = 0.01$

HINT

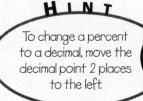

To change a percent to a decimal, move the decimal point 2 places to the left.

Use this pattern:

$100\% = 1.0$ $10\% = 0.10$ $1\% = 0.01$
$0.25\% = 0.0025$

```
 0   0.0025        0.01
 ├─────┼────┼────┼────┤
 0   0.25%          1%
```

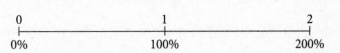

Practice

1. a) Write 175% as a decimal and draw a number line to show this percent.

175% = _____

```
    0                1                2
    ├────────────────┼────────────────┤
   0%              100%             200%
```

b) Write 0.5% as a decimal and draw a number line to show this percent.

0.5% = _____

```
    0              0.01
    ├────┼────┼────┤
    0               1%
```

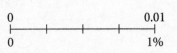

2. Write each percent as a decimal.

    a) 230% _____   **b)** 185% _____   **c)** 324% _____

    d) 0.74% _____   **e)** 0.7% _____   **f)** 0.09% _____

3. Write each fraction as a percent.

    a) $\frac{1}{2}$ _____   **b)** $\frac{3}{2}$ _____   **c)** $\frac{5}{2}$ _____

    d) $\frac{1}{100}$ _____   **e)** $\frac{1}{200}$ _____   **f)** $\frac{3}{200}$ _____

4. a) Find the percent of each number.

    i) 200% of 180   **ii)** 20% of 180   **iii)** 2% of 180

    _____   _____   _____

  b) Use the pattern in part a to find each percent of 180.

    i) 2000% of 180   **ii)** 0.2% of 180

    _____   _____

> **Tip**
>
> *Extend the pattern both ways— increase and decrease by a factor of 10.*

5. In a shipment of 16 000 DVDs, 0.95% were faulty. How many DVDs were faulty?

Write 0.95% as a decimal. 0.95% = _____

0.95% of 16 000 is: _____ × 16 000 = _____

_____ DVDs were faulty.

6. A total of 45 412 runners participated in the Vancouver Sun Run.
Of these runners, 0.85% completed the run in under 40 min.

How many runners completed in under 40 min? _____

In fact, 0.13% of the runners completed the run in less than 34 min.

How many runners were in this group? _____

7. Which is the greater amount of money, 120% of 0.3% of $1000 or 120.3% of $1000?
Explain.

_____

Quick Review

Several hundred students were surveyed. 160 students were from one school.
These students represent 40% of those surveyed.

To find how many students were surveyed, follow these steps:
40% of those surveyed is 160.
1% of those surveyed is $\frac{160}{40} = 4$
100% of those surveyed is $4 \times 100 = 400$

In the next survey, 15% more students were surveyed.
To find the number of students surveyed, use the original number, 160, as 1 whole.

Method 1: The increase was 15%.
The new number is 100% + 15% = 115%.
115% of 160 = $1.15 \times 160 = 184$

Method 2: The increase was 15%. 160 is 100%.
15% of 160 = $0.15 \times 160 = 24$
The new number is: 160 + 24 = 184

> **Tip**
> *Choose the method you feel comfortable using.*

Both methods show that the new number of students surveyed is 184.
This result can be illustrated on a number line.

```
0                    160  184
|--------------------+----+
0%                 100% 115%
```

Practice

1. Find the number in each case.

a) 6% of a number is 9.

    6% = 9

    1% = _____

    100% = _____

b) 28% of a number is 56.

    28% = _____

    1% = _____

    100% = _____

c) 150% of a number is 36.

    150% = _____

    1% = _____

    100% = _____

2. Write each increase or decrease as a percent.

   a) The price of a hotel room increased from $92 to $115.

      Increase = $115 – $92 = _____

      Increase as a fraction of the original = _____ = _____

      Percent increase = _____ × 100% = _____%

   b) The number of students in a class decreased from 30 to 27.

> **Tip**
> Identify which number represents 1 whole, or 100%.

      Percent decrease = _____

   c) The volume of water in a tank decreased from 28 000 L to 26 880 L.

      Percent _____ = _____

   d) The number of employees increased from 725 to 841.

      Percent _____ = _____

3. In a batch of eggs, 3% were broken. There were 18 broken eggs.
How many eggs were there in the batch?

_____

4. The prices for a day pass for skiing are:

Low Season: $52   High Season: $64   Spring Season: $58

   a) Calculate the percent change in cost from Low Season to High Season.

_____

   b) Calculate the percent change in cost from High Season to Spring Season.

_____

5. a) The rural population of Quebec is about 1 650 000. This represents 22% of the population of Quebec. Estimate the population of Quebec.

_____

b) The population of Yukon Territory is about 31 400. Of these, 18 840 live in urban areas. What percent of the population of Yukon Territory lives in rural areas?

_____

6. A fish tank contains 24 L of water. Water is added to increase the volume by 12.5%. What is the new volume of water in the tank?

_____

7. Thirty-six percent of a number is 63. Find 124% of the number.

_____

8. A factory produces 900 items per week at a unit cost of $75. New equipment is installed that increases the productivity by 12% and reduces the production costs by 16%.

a) What is the new production rate?

_____

b) What is the new unit cost?

KEY TO SUCCESS

Problems can always be solved in more than one way. If you cannot solve a problem by one method, look at the problem from another view for an alternative method.

Quick Review

When an item is sold at a reduced price, we say there is a **discount**.
In many provinces, taxes (GST and PST in Ontario) are added to the selling price.
A salesperson earns a **commission** if he/she is paid a percent of the selling price.

Corey works in a shoe store. She has to calculate the cost of a pair of running shoes priced at $129 that is on sale at 20% off.

A discount of 20% means the sale price is:
100% − 20% = 80% of the regular price
80% of $129 = 0.8 × $129 = $103.20
The total sales tax in Corey's province is 14%. The tax is:
14% of $103.20 = 0.14 × $103.20 = $14.45
So, the cost of the running shoes is:
$103.20 + $14.45 = $117.65

> **Tip**
> *Always round money amounts to the nearest hundredth of a dollar.*

This can be calculated directly as: 114% of $103.20 = 1.14 × $103.20 = $117.65

Corey gets 5% commission on the sale of all items in the store.
5% of $103.20 is: 0.05 × $103.20 = $5.16
So, Corey gets $5.16 for the sale of the running shoes.

Practice

1. Calculate a 14% tax on each item.

   a) $288

   b) $36.50

   c) $149.99

   _____ × $288   _____ × _____   _____ × _____

   = _____   = _____   = _____

2. Calculate the cost, including 15% total sales tax, for each item.

   a) $2.40

   b) $3428

   c) $128.79

   _____ × $2.40   _____ × _____   _____ × _____

   = _____   = _____   = _____

3. Calculate each discount and the sale price before tax.

  a) $92 watch, 30% off   **b)** $476 TV, 15% off

  Discount: _____   Discount: _____

  Sale price: _____   Sale price: _____

4. Bill earns 4% commission on sales up to and including $25 000, and 6% commission on all sales over $25 000. How much commission will he earn on sales of $80 000?

  First part of commission: 4% of $25 000 = _____

  Second part of commission: 6% of $_____ = _____

                                                = _____

  Total commission = _____

5. The price of a house is reduced from $425 000 to $374 000.

  a) What is the percent decrease? _____

  b) Calculate the sale price, including 15% tax. _____

6. At a discount of 25%, skateboards are on sale for $135. What is the original price?

  HINT

  To find 100%, first find 1%.

  The original price is _____.

7. Store A offers successive discounts of 10% one week and 20% the second week. Store B offers a one-time discount of 25% the second week.

  Which store offers in the greater discount? _____

8. A TV set, regularly priced at $256, is offered for sale at 25% off. Sales tax is 15%.
  a) Calculate the sale price at 25% discount and then add 15% sales tax to it.
  b) Add 15% tax to the original price and then calculate the sale price at 25% discount.

  Which calculation results in the greater discount? _____

Quick Review

Interest is the money you pay for borrowing money, or the money you earn by investing.

For example, at an annual interest rate of 8%,
the interest on $100 for 1 year is: 0.08 × $100 = $8
the interest on $100 for 3 years is: 3 × 0.08 × $100 = $24
the interest on $500 for 3 years is: 3 × 0.08 × $500 = $120

This type of interest is called **simple interest**.
It can be calculated using the formula: $I = Prt$
I is the simple interest.
P is the **principal**, or the money, borrowed or invested.
r is the annual interest rate as a decimal.
t is the time in years.

So, the simple interest, I, on $800 invested at an annual interest rate of 6% for 4 months is:
$Prt = \$800 \times 0.06 \times \frac{3}{12} = \$12$
The **amount** received after 4 months is: principal + interest = $800 + $12 = $812

Practice

1. Write each percent as a decimal.

   a) 7% _____   **b)** 4.9% _____   **c)** $3\frac{1}{2}$% _____   **d)** $4\frac{3}{4}$% _____

2. Express each time period as a fraction of 1 year.

   a) 6 months _____   **b)** 9 months _____   **c)** 15 months _____

3. Calculate the simple interest for $700 invested at an annual interest rate of 5% for 4 years.

   The interest on $100 for 1 year is: _____ × $100 = _____

   The interest on $100 for 4 years is: 4 × _____ × $100 = _____

   The interest on $700 for 4 years is: 4 × _____ × _____ = _____

4. Calculate the simple interest paid on each deposit.

Deposit	Annual Interest Rate	Time (years)	Simple Interest
$500	6%	5	$150
$1150	4.5%	4	$207
$5000	3.5%	2.5	$437.50

5. Joshua borrows $3000 for 4 years at an annual simple interest rate of 8%.
He agrees to pay back the money in equal monthly installments over the 4 years.

 a) What simple interest will Joshua pay? _____

 b) What amount will Joshua have to pay back? _____

 c) How much will he pay back each month? _____

6. Kelsie has an $800 savings bond which she has had for $2\frac{1}{2}$ years.
The bond pays simple interest at the rate of 3.8% per year.
If Kelsie cashes the bond, what amount will she receive?

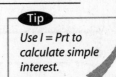

Tip

Use I = Prt to calculate simple interest.

Kelsie will receive _____.

7. Grace borrowed $2560 at an interest rate of 4.75% per year.
She agrees to pay back the money after 9 months, including interest.
What amount will she have to pay back?

Grace will have to pay back _____.

8. Pete borrowed $400 for one year. He paid back a total of $440.
What was the interest rate per year?

HINT

Work backward. Find the interest paid, then find the interest rate.

The interest rate was _____ per year.

In Your Words

Here are some of the important mathematical words of this unit.
Build your own glossary by recording definitions and examples here. The first one is done for you.

proportion _a statement that 2 ratios are equal_

For example, $\frac{x}{3} = \frac{11}{15}$

The value of an unknown x can be found by solving the proportion:

$3 \times \frac{x}{3} = \frac{11}{15} \times 3, x = 2.2$

unit rate

sales tax

discount

commission

simple interest

List other mathematical words you need to know.

Unit Review

LESSON

2.1 **1.** At a summer camp, for every 3 students who sailed, 5 kayaked.
Forty-five students kayaked. How many students sailed?

Let *s* be the number of students who sailed. Write a proportion.

s:number of students kayaked = _____:_____

> **Tip**
> Writing the variable as the first term in the ratio makes it easier to solve the proportion.

_____ students sailed.

2. In a bag of coloured cubes, the ratio of red cubes to total number of cubes is 5:7.
If there are 105 cubes in the bag, how many cubes are red?

_____ cubes are red.

3. At a school outing, the ratio of boys to girls is 3:4.
If 84 students went on the outing, how many students were girls?

_____ students were girls.

2.2 **4.** The scale of a map is 1:6 000 000.

a) The distance between 2 towns on the map is 8.7 cm. What is the actual distance?

1 cm on the map represents _____ cm actual distance.

The actual distance between the 2 towns is:

_____ × _____ cm = _____ cm = _____ km

b) The distance between 2 other towns is 1248 km. What is the distance on the map?

_____

5. A model plane is built to a scale of 1:60.
What is the wingspan of the model if the plane has a wingspan of 58.5 m?

_____

6. A beetle is 1.8 cm long. A drawing of the beetle is made using a scale of 5:1.
What is the length of the beetle in the drawing?

_____

2.3 **7.** Which is the better buy?
2.9 L of detergent for $4.56 or 3.8 L for $5.78

_____

8. A cruise ship travelled 84 km in 3.5 h.
At this rate, how long will it take to travel 1050 km?

_____

9. Which country has the greater population density? Write its population density.
The United Kingdom with about 60 million people and an area of 244 800 km^2
or China with about 1806 million people and an area of 9 590 000 km^2

_____

2.4 **10.** Write each fraction as a decimal and as a percent.

a) $\frac{4}{5}$ = _____

= _____

b) $\frac{8}{5}$ = _____

= _____

c) $\frac{3}{1000}$ = _____

= _____

d) $\frac{15}{6000}$ = _____

= _____

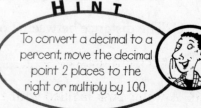

H I N T

To convert a decimal to a percent, move the decimal point 2 places to the right or multiply by 100.

11. In a sponsored walk for charity, 560 students participated.
Of these, 0.72% completed the 15-km walk. How many students completed this distance?

_____

12. Calculate 0.76% of 150% of 6000.

_____

13. In 1895, the population of a small town was 2120.
By 1905, the population increased to 115% of the 1895 figure.

a) What was the population in 1905?

_____

b) Find the increase in population from 1895 to 1905.

_____

2.5   **14.** Find the amount in each case.

a) 8% is 56 kg.   **b)** 125% is 85 cm.   **c)** 0.48% is 84 L.

_____   _____   _____

15. Write each increase or decrease as a percent.

a) The price of gasoline rose from 97.5¢/L to 101.4¢/L.

Percent increase = _____

b) The number of trucks crossing the border fell from 3240 to 2673.

Percent decrease = _____

16. A water tank is filled with 1500 L of water. In one hour, the tank loses 5.4% of the water
due to leakage. What is the volume of water in the tank after one hour?

_____

2.6

17. The tax rate is 14%. Calculate the selling price of each item before and after tax.

  a) $125 item at 10% off   **b)** $1820 item at 25% off   **c)** $6.80 item at 15% off

  Before: _____   Before: _____   Before: _____

  After: _____   After: _____   After: _____

18. Janine is paid commission of 3% on all sales up to and including $10 000, and 5% on all sales over $10 000. How much commission will she earn on sales of $48 000?

> **Tip**
> *The commission consists of 2 parts.*

_____

19. The sale price of a computer at 15% off is $746.30. What is the regular price?

_____

20. A store owner buys coats for $56 each. She adds 30% to the cost and sells the coats at 15% off. Find the selling price of each coat.

_____

2.7

21. Find the simple interest paid on each deposit.

> **Tip**
> *Use the formula I = Prt to calculate simple interest.*

  a) $3800 at an annual rate of 3.5% for 3 years

  _____

  b) $500 000 at an annual rate of 5.6% for 9 months

  _____

22. Moshe borrows $3250 at a simple interest rate of 6.4% per year for 2 years. He agrees to pay back the money in equal monthly payments over the 2 years.

  a) What simple interest will he pay? _____

  b) What is each monthly installment? _____

23. Enid has a $1500 savings bond which she has had for 2.5 years. The bond pays simple interest of 4% per year. If she cashes the bond, what amount will she receive?

_____

Geometry and Measurement

Just for Fun

Word Search Riddle

What will an acorn say to itself when it grows up?

____ ____ ____ ____ ____ ____ ____ ____

To solve the riddle, follow these steps:

1. Find the list of words in the word search table on the right.
    Words can be horizontal, vertical, or diagonal.

AREA, BASE, CUBIC, EDGE,

EULER, FORMULA, HEIGHT,

ISOMETRIC, MEASUREMENT,

NET, PICTORIAL, PRISM,

RECTANGULAR, SOLVE,

SQUARE, SUBSTITUTE, SUM,

SURFACE, TRIANGULAR,

VERTICAL, VERTICES,

VIEW, VOLUME

T	E	G	I	S	O	M	E	T	R	I	C
H	R	E	C	T	A	N	G	U	L	A	R
G	A	I	P	I	C	T	O	R	I	A	L
I	U	S	A	G	F	O	R	M	U	L	A
E	Q	U	E	N	E	M	U	L	O	V	A
H	S	R	C	F	G	O	S	V	I	E	W
B	M	F	U	Y	D	U	O	U	R	R	P
E	S	A	B	E	E	P	L	A	M	T	R
L	A	C	I	T	R	E	V	A	T	I	I
T	R	E	C	E	U	L	E	R	R	C	S
R	T	N	E	M	E	R	U	S	A	E	M
N	E	T	U	T	I	T	S	B	U	S	Y

2. Write all unused letters in order, row by row, from left to right.

_____

3. Cross out every second letter to solve the riddle.

_____

Skills You'll Need

Drawing Isometric and Pictorial Diagrams

An **isometric diagram** is a drawing on isometric (triangular) dot paper that shows the three dimensions of an object. The three-dimensional effect is created by shading the visible faces differently.

A **pictorial diagram** is a drawing with the depth of an object drawn to a smaller scale than its length and width. The different scales visually create a three-dimensional effect.

Example 1

a) Make an isometric diagram of this object.

b) Make a pictorial diagram of this object.

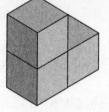

Solution

a) Follow these steps on isometric paper:

Join 2 dots for each vertical edge.	Join a pair of dots diagonally for each horizontal edge that goes up to the right.	Join a pair of dots diagonally for each horizontal edge that goes up to the left.

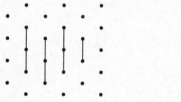 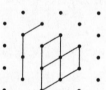 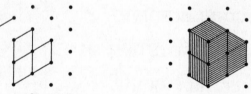

Shade the faces to give a three-dimensional look.

b) Use the congruent opposite faces of the object as the front and back faces.
Draw the front face.
Then draw its translation image.
Join the corresponding vertices to give a three-dimensional look.

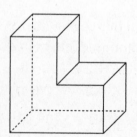

Use broken lines to show hidden edges.

1. Make an isometric diagram and a pictorial diagram of a square prism with dimensions 3 units by 3 units by 2 units.

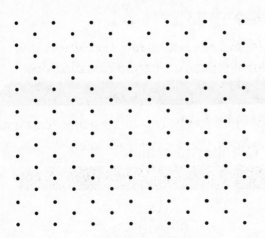

2. Make a pictorial diagram of a lamp shade.

Calculating the Surface Area and Volume of a Rectangular Prism

A rectangular prism has 6 faces. The opposite faces of the prism are congruent.

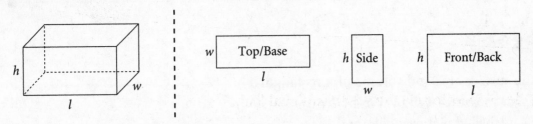

The surface area of a rectangular prism is the sum of the areas of the 6 faces.

Surface area = 2 × area of base + 2 × area of side face + 2 × area of front face

Using symbols: $SA = 2 \times (l \times w) + 2 \times (h \times w) + 2 \times (l \times h)$

$$SA = 2lw + 2hw + 2lh$$

The formula for surface area is: $SA = 2(lw + hw + lh)$

In this formula, l is the length, w is the width, and h is the height.

The volume of a rectangular prism is the product of the area of base and height.

The formula for volume is: $V = lwh$

A cube is a rectangular prism that has 6 square faces. That is, $l = w = h$.
So, the formula for surface area and volume can be simplified.

Area of each face: $s \times s = s^2$
Surface area: $SA = 6s^2$

Volume: $V = s \times s \times s = s^3$

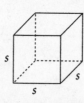

Example 2

A rectangular prism has dimensions 7 cm by 6 cm by 4 cm.

a) Calculate the surface area.   **b)** Calculate the volume.

Solution

Draw and label a pictorial diagram.

a) Use the formula for the surface area
of a rectangular prism:
$SA = 2(lw + hw + lh)$
Substitute $l = 7$, $w = 6$, and $h = 4$.
$SA = 2[(7 \times 6) + (4 \times 6) + (7 \times 4)]$
$ = 2(42 + 24 + 28) = 2(94) = 188$
The surface area is 188 cm².

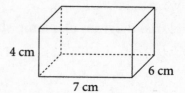

b) Use the formula for the volume of a rectangular prism: $V = lwh$
Substitute $l = 7$, $w = 6$, and $h = 4$.
$V = 7 \times 6 \times 4 = 168$
The volume is 168 cm³.

✓ Check

3. Find the surface area and volume of a rectangular
prism that measures 4 m by 3 m by 2 m.
Include a labelled pictorial diagram.

$SA = 2(lw + hw + lh)$

Substitute $l = $ _____, $w = $ _____, and $h = $ _____.

$SA = 2[(\underline{\hspace{1cm}} \times \underline{\hspace{1cm}}) + (\underline{\hspace{1cm}} \times \underline{\hspace{1cm}}) + (\underline{\hspace{1cm}} \times \underline{\hspace{1cm}})]$

$= \underline{\hspace{6cm}}$

The surface area is _____ m².

50

$$V = lwh = \underline{\hspace{1cm}} \times \underline{\hspace{1cm}} \times \underline{\hspace{1cm}} = \underline{\hspace{1cm}}$$

The volume is \underline{\hspace{3cm}} m³.

4. Find the surface area and volume of each rectangular prism.

a) 15 mm by 15 mm by 6 mm

b) 1.2 cm by 1.2 cm by 1.2 cm

Surface area: \underline{\hspace{4cm}}

Surface area: \underline{\hspace{4cm}}

Volume: \underline{\hspace{3cm}}

Volume: \underline{\hspace{3cm}}

Calculating the Area of a Triangle

To calculate the area of a triangle, use either of these formulas:
Area = base × height ÷ 2   or   Area = $\frac{1}{2}$ × base × height

Using symbols: $A = \frac{bh}{2}$ or $A = \frac{1}{2}bh$

where b is the base length and h is the corresponding height.

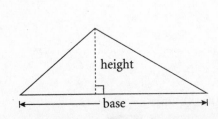 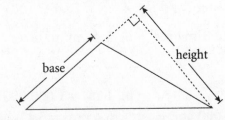

Example 3

Calculate the area of this triangle.

Solution

Use the formula $A = \frac{bh}{2}$
Substitute $b = 7.8$ and $h = 1.8$.
$A = \frac{bh}{2} = \frac{7.8 \times 1.8}{2} = 7.02$

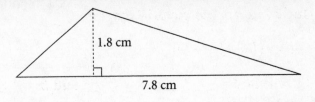

The area is about 7 cm² to the nearest square centimetre.

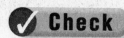

5. Calculate the area of each triangle.

a) $A = \frac{bh}{2} = \underline{\hspace{3cm}}$
$$ \qquad \qquad 2$$

$= \underline{\hspace{3cm}}$

The area is \underline{\hspace{3cm}} m².

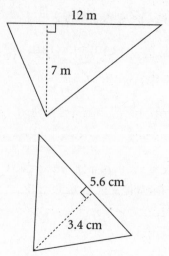

b) $A = \frac{bh}{2}$

The area is \underline{\hspace{3cm}}.

Converting among Units of Measure

$1 \text{ m}^2 = 1 \text{ m} \times 1 \text{ m} = 100 \text{ cm} \times 100 \text{ cm} = 10\ 000 \text{ cm}^2$, or 10^4 cm^2

$1 \text{ m}^3 = 1 \text{ m} \times 1 \text{ m} \times 1 \text{ m} = 100 \text{ cm} \times 100 \text{ cm} \times 100 \text{ cm} = 1\ 000\ 000 \text{ cm}^3$, or 10^6 cm^3

$1 \text{ cm}^3 = 1 \text{ mL}$ $\qquad\qquad$ $1000 \text{ cm}^3 = 1000 \text{ mL} = 1 \text{ L}$

Example 4

Convert.

a) 5.6 m² to square centimetres b) 5.43 m³ to litres

Solution

a) $1 \text{ m}^2 = 10\ 000 \text{ cm}^2$
$5.6 \text{ m}^2 = 5.6 \times 10\ 000 \text{ cm}^2$
$\qquad\quad = 56\ 000 \text{ cm}^2$

b) $1 \text{ m}^3 = 1\ 000\ 000 \text{ cm}^3$
$5.43 \text{ m}^3 = 5.43 \times 1\ 000\ 000 \text{ cm}^3$
$\qquad\qquad = 5\ 430\ 000 \text{ cm}^3$
$1000 \text{ cm}^3 = 1 \text{ L}$
$5\ 430\ 000 \text{ cm}^3 = \frac{5\ 430\ 000}{1000} \text{ L}$
$\qquad\qquad\qquad = 5430 \text{ L}$

Tip

To divide by 1000, move the decimal point 3 places to the left.

6. Convert.

a) 2600 cm² to square metres

b) 4.7 L to cubic centimetres

Quick Review

➤ Each view of an object is a two-dimensional drawing that gives information about the shape of the object.

The top, front, and side views are often enough to identify or build the object. In the diagram, these 3 views of an object are shown.

The top view is a trapezoid.
The side view is a rectangle.
The front view is 3 rectangles, 2 of which are congruent.

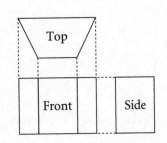

Trapezoidal
Prism

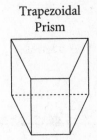

These views match the object on the right.
So, the object is identified as a trapezoidal prism.

➤ You can sketch an object built using linking cubes when different views are given. An internal line segment shows where the depth or thickness of the object changes.

Views of object on grid paper: Sketch of object on isometric paper:

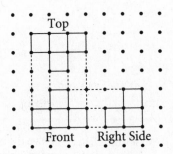

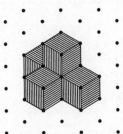

The top and front views show that the object has a row of 3 cubes at the bottom layer.
The top and right side views show that 1 cube sticks out from the middle of the 3 cubes.
The internal lines show that there is a second layer of 1 cube in the middle.
So, the object has 5 linking cubes arranged as sketched on isometric paper.

Practice

Use linking cubes if needed.

1. Name the object that has each set of views.

a) _____

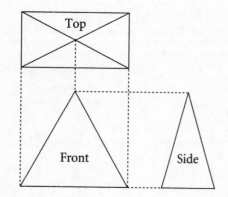

H I N T

Remember that internal line segments show where the depth or thickness of the object changes.

b) _____   c) _____

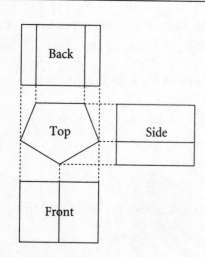

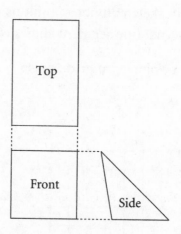

2. Complete this table for objects in question 1 to check Euler's formula.

Object	Vertices (*V*)	Faces (*F*)	Edges (*E*)	$V + F - E =$
a)			8	
b)		7		
c)	6			

State Euler's formula. _____

54

3. The front view of this object is given. Sketch 2 other views.

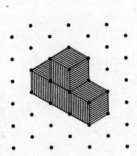

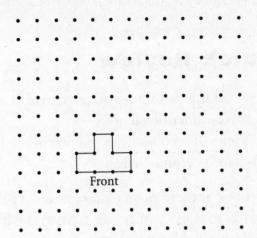

Front

4. a) Use these views to build an object.   **b)** Sketch the object on isometric dot paper.

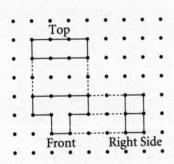

Top

Front   Right Side

5. a) Use these views to build an object.   **b)** Sketch the object on isometric dot paper.

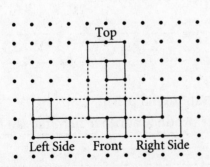

Top

Left Side   Front   Right Side

Quick Review

➤ A net is a two-dimensional pattern that can be folded into a three-dimensional object.
Views of an object can provide information on the number of faces and which faces share a common edge.

➤ Look at these views of a trapezoidal prism. You may use a ruler and 1-cm grid paper to draw a net for the object.

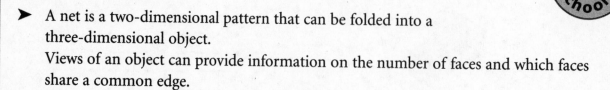

Use the top view to draw the first face A. Then draw connecting faces.

The front view shows 3 rectangular faces that are joined to the top face.
These 3 rectangular faces must have dimensions that match the dimensions at the shared edges.

So, the front rectangle B is 2 cm by 3 cm. Each side rectangle C is 2.2 cm by 3 cm.

The views do not show the back face and the bottom face.

Since this is a prism, the bottom face D is congruent to the top face A, with its 2-cm edge connecting the bottom edge of the front face B.

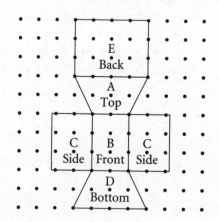

The dimensions of the back face E can be determined using the dimensions of its connecting faces.
So, rectangle E is 4 cm by 3 cm.

➤ This is not the only net you can draw for this trapezoidal prism.
Different arrangements of the same 6 faces may produce another net that can be folded to give the same prism.

To check if another arrangement is also a net for the prism, cut out the figure and fold to form the object.

Practice

1. These views represent an object. Identify the object and draw a possible net.

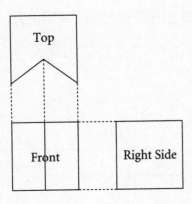

The object is a _____.

2. These views represent an object. Identify the object and draw a possible net. Then describe the object.

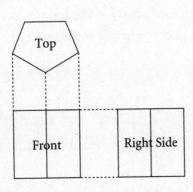

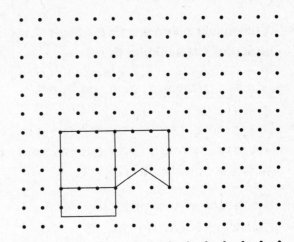

_____

_____

Quick Review

➤ A triangular prism is a three-dimensional figure with 2 congruent, triangular faces and 3 rectangular faces.

Here is a triangular prism and its net.

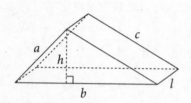
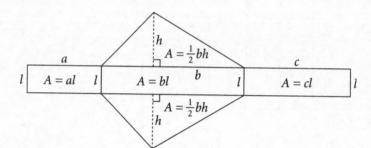

➤ You can use the net of the triangular prism to find the surface area of the prism. The surface area, *SA*, is the sum of the areas of all the faces.

In a word formula:
SA = sum of the areas of 3 rectangular faces + 2 × area of 1 triangular face

In symbols:
$SA = al + bl + cl + 2 \times \frac{1}{2}bh$ or $SA = al + bl + cl + bh$
where *a*, *b*, and *c* are the 3 side lengths of the triangular faces, *l* is the length of the prism, and *h* is the height of the triangular face that corresponds to the base *b*.

Practice

1. Calculate the area of this net.

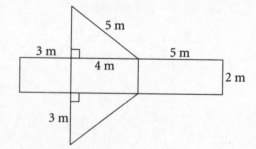

   Length of prism: *l* = _____

   The 3 sides of a triangular face:

   a = _____, *b* = _____, *c* = _____

   Height of prism: *h* = _____

   Substitute each variable in the formula: *SA* = *al* + *bl* + *cl* + *bh*

   SA = _____ + _____ + _____ + _____ = _____

   The area of the net is _____ m².

2. Calculate the surface area of each prism. Draw a net first if it helps.

a) Identify the variable that represents each dimension.

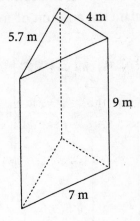

$l =$ _____ $h =$ _____

$a =$ _____ $b =$ _____ $c =$ _____

$SA =$ _____ + _____ +

_____ + _____

$=$ _____

The area of the prism is _____ m².

b)

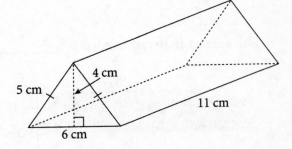

The area of the prism is _____ cm².

3. The area of each triangular face of this prism is 7.5 m².
Calculate the surface area of the prism. Show your work.

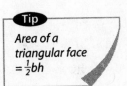

Tip

Area of a triangular face $= \frac{1}{2}bh$

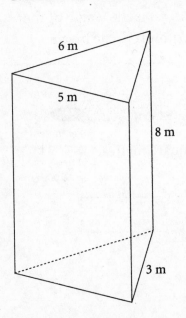

The area of the prism is _____ m².

4. A packing company is making these containers.
A shaded region indicates that the face is not needed for the container.
Calculate the amount of material needed to make each. Show your work.

a)

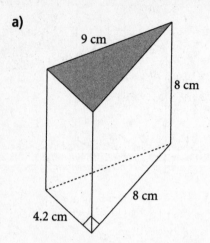

The area of material needed is _____ cm².

b)

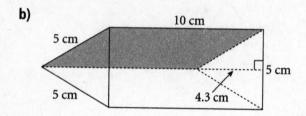

The area of material needed is _____ cm².

5. A triangular prism has a base with a perimeter 36 cm and area 54 cm².

   a) The length of the prism is 24 cm. Find its surface area in square metres.

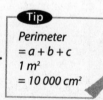

Perimeter
= a + b + c
1 m²
= 10 000 cm²

   b) Suppose the base of the prism is a right triangle.
   Suggest possible whole-number dimensions for the base.

Quick Review

At Home At School

In this diagram, the rectangular prism and triangular prism have the same length. Both the rectangular face and the triangular face have the same base and height.

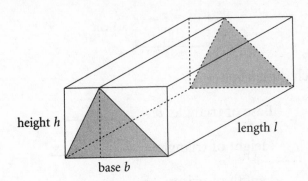

height *h*

base *b*

length *l*

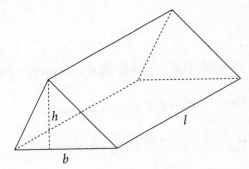

h

b

l

You know that the volume of a rectangular prism is: *V* = base area × length

In symbols: $V = b \times h \times l$, where *b* is the base and *h* is the height of the rectangular face, and *l* is the length of the prism

From the diagram, the volume of the triangular prism of the same base, height, and length is one-half the volume of the rectangular prism.

So, the volume of a triangular prism is: $V = \frac{1}{2} \times b \times h \times l$

Since the area of a triangle is one-half the area of a rectangle of the same base and height, the volume of a triangular prism is also: *V* = base area × length

In symbols: $V = \frac{1}{2}bh \times l$, or $V = \frac{1}{2}bhl$

Practice

1. The base area and length for this triangular prism is given.
   Find its volume.

   V = base area × length

   = _____ × _____

   = _____

   The volume of the triangular prism is _____ m³.

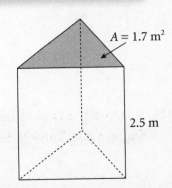

$A = 1.7\ m^2$

2.5 m

61

2. Find the volume of each triangular prism to the nearest cubic centimetre.

a)

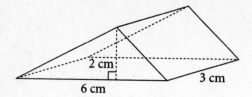

b)

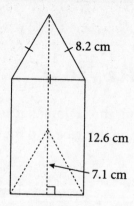

Identify the variable that represents each dimension.

Base of triangle: $b =$ _____   Base of triangle: $b =$ _____

Height of triangle: $h =$ _____   Height of triangle: $h =$ _____

Length of prism: $l =$ _____   Length of prism: $l =$ _____

Volume of prism: $V = \frac{1}{2}bhl$ Volume of prism: $V = \frac{1}{2}bhl$

$V =$ _____ $V =$ _____

The volume is _____.   The volume is _____.

3. Calculate the volume of each triangular prism to the nearest cubic metre.

a)

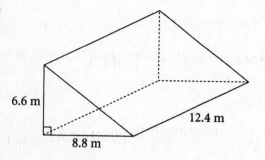

b)

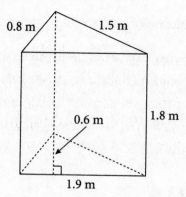

The volume is _____.   The volume is _____.

4. A company packages candies in triangular prisms.
Each box contains 120 cm³ of candy.
The diagram shows the shape of the container box.

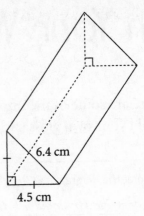

6.4 cm

4.5 cm

a) How long is the box to the nearest centimetre?

The length of the box is about _____ cm.

b) How much material would it take to make this container?

The container needs _____ of material.

5. If the company in question 4 doubled the dimensions of
the triangular face but not the length, estimate the
volume of the new container. Explain your estimate.
Include a sketch of the new prism.
Calculate the new volume to check your estimate.

In Your Words

Here are some of the important words of this unit.
Build your own glossary by recording definitions and examples here. The first one is done for you.

isometric diagram _drawing on isometric (triangular) dot paper that shows the three dimensions of an object. For example, this is an isometric diagram of a cube._

net _____

triangular prism _____

surface area _____

volume _____

view _____

List other mathematical words you need to know.

_____

Unit Review

LESSON

3.1 **1. a)** Use these views to build an object.

b) Sketch the object on isometric dot paper.

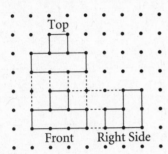

3.2 **2.** These views represent an object. Identify the object and draw a possible net.

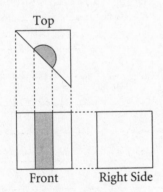

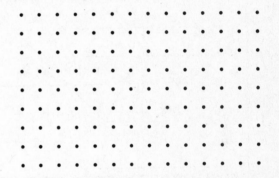

A shaded region is an opening in a face.

Describe the object.

_____

_____

_____

_____

_____

3. Calculate the surface area and volume of each triangular prism.

a)

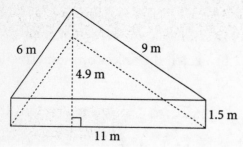

6 m   9 m

4.9 m

1.5 m

11 m

_____

b)

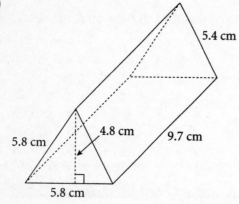

5.4 cm

4.8 cm

5.8 cm   9.7 cm

5.8 cm

_____

4. A triangular prism has volume 75 m² and a right triangular base of area 10 m².

    a) What is the length of the prism?

_____

    b) Sketch a possible prism.
    Label its dimensions.

UNIT 4

Fractions and Decimals

Just for Fun

A Game for 2 or more

Box It!

Take turns drawing a line connecting any two dots. The lines may be horizontal or vertical, but not diagonal.

When you complete a box, write your initials in it.

Play until all the dots are used.

The player whose initials are in the most boxes wins.

Fraction Word Search

Can you find this list of words in the word search table at the right?

Words can be horizontal, vertical, or diagonal.

SIMPLIFY   FRACTION

IMPROPER   MIXED

NUMERATOR   PART

EQUIVALENT   WHOLE

K	V	W	W	X	J	J	O	S	E
F	Q	P	U	K	M	P	P	Q	W
R	O	T	A	R	E	M	U	N	V
A	E	T	W	W	F	I	U	Z	X
C	D	P	H	P	V	X	Y	A	M
T	K	H	O	A	Q	E	N	N	L
I	E	Z	L	R	E	D	W	F	G
O	M	E	E	T	P	U	Z	M	Q
N	N	E	W	F	O	M	H	W	I
T	C	S	I	M	P	L	I	F	Y

Skills You'll Need

Multiply a Fraction by a Whole Number

The $\times$ symbol means "groups of."

$3 \times \frac{1}{2}$ means 3 groups of $\frac{1}{2}$.

$\frac{1}{2} \times 3$ means one-half of a group of 3, or $\frac{1}{2}$ of 3.

In each case, the product is 3 halves, or $\frac{3}{2}$.

$3 \times \frac{1}{2} = \frac{3}{2}$

$\frac{1}{2} \times 3 = \frac{3}{2}$

Example

a) Find $\frac{2}{3}$ of 4.

b) Find $2 \times \frac{5}{6}$.

Solution

a) $\frac{2}{3}$ of 4 is $\frac{2}{3} \times 4$.

$\frac{2}{3} \times 4 = \frac{2 \times 4}{3}$

$= \frac{8}{3}$

b) $2 \times \frac{5}{6} = \frac{2 \times 5}{6}$

$= \frac{10}{6}$

$= \frac{10 \div 2}{6 \div 2}$

$= \frac{5}{3}$

HINT

A fraction is in simplest form when the GCF of the numerator and denominator is 1.

✓ Check

1. Match all three columns. The first one is done for you.

$\frac{1}{2}$ of 6	$\frac{5}{2} \times 8$	$\frac{6}{5}$
3 groups of $\frac{2}{5}$	$6 \times \frac{2}{3}$	3
6 groups of $\frac{2}{3}$	$\frac{1}{2} \times 6$	4
$\frac{5}{2}$ of 8	$3 \times \frac{2}{5}$	20

2. Rajah has read $\frac{3}{4}$ of a 120-page book. How many pages has he read? _____

$\frac{3}{4}$ of 120 = _____

68

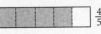

Quick Review

➤ When two fractions have the same denominator, the greater fraction has the greater numerator.

There are more fifths in $\frac{4}{5}$ than in $\frac{2}{5}$.

So, $\frac{4}{5} > \frac{2}{5}$.

$\frac{4}{5}$

$\frac{2}{5}$

➤ To compare fractions with different denominators:
* Use the lowest common multiple of the denominators as the common denominator.
* Find equivalent fractions with the same denominator and compare numerators.

Which is smaller, $\frac{2}{3}$ or $\frac{5}{7}$?
Multiples of 3 are: 3, 6, 9, 12, 15, 18, **21**, 24, . . .
Multiples of 7 are: 7, 14, **21**, 28, . . .
The lowest common multiple of 3 and 7 is 21.
Write equivalent fractions for $\frac{2}{3}$ and $\frac{5}{7}$ with denominator 21.

> **Tip**
> When the denominators have no factors in common, the lowest common multiple is their product:
> $3 \times 7 = 21$

$$\overset{\times\,7}{\underset{\times\,7}{\frac{2}{3} = \frac{14}{21}}} \qquad \overset{\times\,3}{\underset{\times\,3}{\frac{5}{7} = \frac{15}{21}}}$$

Compare the numerators.

Since $14 < 15$, $\frac{14}{21} < \frac{15}{21}$, or $\frac{2}{3} < \frac{5}{7}$.

Practice

1. Write an equivalent fraction with the given denominator.

a) $$\overset{\times\,4}{\underset{\times\,4}{\frac{2}{5} = \frac{}{20}}}$$

b) $$\overset{\times\,\mathbf{6}}{\underset{\times\,6}{\frac{3}{4} = \frac{}{24}}}$$

c) $\frac{7}{12} = \frac{}{36}$

2. Find the greater fraction in each pair.

a) $\frac{2}{5}, \frac{1}{3}$

5 and 3 have no factors in common.

The lowest common multiple of 5 and 3 is _____.

Write equivalent fractions with this as the denominator.

$\frac{2}{5} = \frac{\quad\quad}{15}$ $\qquad\qquad$ $\frac{1}{3} = $ _____

HINT

When the denominators are the same, compare the numerators.

_____ is the greater fraction.

b) $\frac{3}{5}, \frac{3}{4}$ _____

c) $\frac{5}{9}, \frac{2}{3}$ _____

d) $\frac{3}{7}, \frac{2}{5}$ _____

3. Write a fraction halfway between each pair of fractions.

a) $\frac{12}{6}, \frac{12}{4}$ _____

b) $\frac{2}{5}, \frac{5}{10}$ _____

Tip

Sometimes, you need to use a greater common multiple as the common denominator.

4. Order $\frac{2}{9}, \frac{1}{6},$ and $\frac{1}{4}$ from least to greatest.

Multiples of 9 are: _____ Multiples of 6 are: _____

Multiples of 4 are: _____

The lowest common multiple of 9, 6, and 4 is: _____

$\frac{2}{9} = $ _____ $\qquad$ $\frac{1}{6} = $ _____ $\qquad$ $\frac{1}{4} = $ _____

From least to greatest: _____.

5. Four friends were practicing basketball free throws. Here are the results.

a) Order the fractions from greatest to least.

_____

Player	Maria	Ed	Sumi	Lucy
Shots made / Shots attempted	$\frac{2}{3}$	$\frac{7}{9}$	$\frac{5}{6}$	$\frac{3}{4}$

b) List the players from the most accurate to the least accurate.

_____

Quick Review

➤ To add fractions with the same denominator, add the numerators.

1 fifth + 2 fifths = 3 fifths

$$\frac{1}{5} + \frac{2}{5} = \frac{3}{5}$$

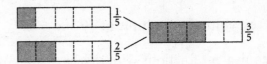

Then write the sum over the common denominator.

➤ To add fractions with different denominators:
  • Use the lowest common multiple of the denominators as the common denominator.
  • Write equivalent fractions with this common denominator.

To add $\frac{1}{4}$ and $\frac{5}{6}$, find the lowest common multiple of 4 and 6.

Multiples of 4 are: 4, 8, **12**, 16, . . .   Multiples of 6 are: 6, **12**, 18, . . .

The lowest common multiple of 4 and 6 is 12.

Write equivalent fractions using 12 as the denominator.

$$\overset{\times 3}{\frac{1}{4} = \frac{3}{12}} \qquad \overset{\times 2}{\frac{5}{6} = \frac{10}{12}}$$
$$\underset{\times 3}{} \qquad \underset{\times 2}{}$$

$$\frac{1}{4} + \frac{5}{6} = \frac{3}{12} + \frac{10}{12} = \frac{13}{12}$$

➤ To add mixed numbers, add the fractions and then add the whole numbers together. Simplify if necessary.

$$2\frac{1}{4} + 3\frac{5}{6} = 2\frac{3}{12} + 3\frac{10}{12}$$
$$= 5\frac{13}{12}$$
$$= 5 + 1\frac{1}{12}$$
$$= 6\frac{1}{12}$$

H I N T

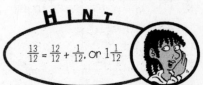

$\frac{13}{12} = \frac{12}{12} + \frac{1}{12}$, or $1\frac{1}{12}$

1. Add. $\frac{7}{10} + \frac{1}{6}$

   Multiples of 10 are: _____

   Multiples of 6 are: _____

   The lowest common multiple of 10 and 6 is: _____

   Write equivalent fractions with this as the denominator.

   $\frac{7}{10} + \frac{1}{6} =$ _____ + _____

   $=$ _____

   $=$ _____

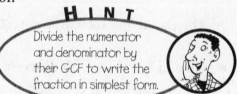

HINT

Divide the numerator and denominator by their GCF to write the fraction in simplest form.

2. Add. Write the answer in simplest form.

   a) $\frac{3}{10} + \frac{1}{2} =$ _____

   b) $\frac{1}{2} + \frac{3}{7} =$ _____

   c) $\frac{3}{10} + \frac{4}{7} =$ _____

   d) $\frac{3}{4} + \frac{5}{6} + \frac{1}{3} =$ _____

3. Complete this magic square so that the sum of every row, column, and diagonal is 1. Write all fractions in simplest form.

$\frac{8}{15}$	$\frac{1}{15}$	
	$\frac{1}{3}$	

key to success

During a test/an exam, read over all questions before you start to answer. Start with those questions that you know how to answer first.

4. Add. Write the answer as a mixed number in simplest form.

a) $3\frac{1}{3} + 4\frac{1}{2}$

    $\frac{1}{3} + \frac{1}{2} =$ _____

    $3 + 4 =$ _____

    So, $3\frac{1}{3} + 4\frac{1}{2} =$ _____

b) $2\frac{5}{6} + 1\frac{3}{8}$

    So, $2\frac{5}{6} + 1\frac{3}{8} =$ _____

HINT

Write the sum of $\frac{5}{6}$ and $\frac{3}{8}$ as a mixed number.

5. Khalid ate $\frac{1}{3}$ of a pizza and his sister ate $\frac{1}{4}$ of it.

a) What fraction of the pizza did they eat together? Show your work.

_____

b) How many slices could there be in the pizza?

_____

6. Last week, Jenna worked $5\frac{2}{3}$ h babysitting and $3\frac{1}{2}$ h giving swimming lessons. How many hours did she work in all?

_____

Quick Review

The strategies for subtracting fractions are similar to those for adding fractions.

➤ If the denominators are the same, subtract the numerators.
Then write the difference over the common denominator.

4 fifths – 1 fifth = 3 fifths

$$\frac{4}{5} - \frac{1}{5} = \frac{3}{5}$$

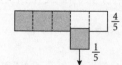

➤ If the denominators are different, subtract equivalent fractions with the same denominator.

To subtract $\frac{1}{2} - \frac{1}{8}$, find the lowest common multiple of 2 and 8.

The lowest common multiple of 2 and 8 is 8.

Write equivalent fractions using 8 as the denominator.

> **Tip**
>
> *Since 8 is a multiple of 2, it is the lowest common multiple of 2 and 8.*

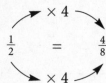

$$\frac{1}{2} = \frac{4}{8}$$

So, $\frac{1}{2} - \frac{1}{8} = \frac{4}{8} - \frac{1}{8}$

$$= \frac{3}{8}$$

➤ To subtract mixed numbers, subtract the fractions and then subtract the whole numbers. Sometimes, you need to regroup a whole number to subtract the fractions.

$$5\frac{1}{8} - 3\frac{1}{2} = 5\frac{1}{8} - 3\frac{4}{8}$$

$$= 4\frac{9}{8} - 3\frac{4}{8}$$

$$= 1\frac{5}{8}$$

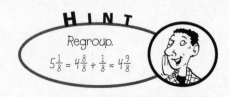

HINT

Regroup.

$5\frac{1}{8} = 4\frac{8}{8} + \frac{1}{8} = 4\frac{9}{8}$

1. Subtract. $\frac{3}{4} - \frac{3}{10}$

   Multiples of 4 are: _____

   Multiples of 10 are: _____

   The lowest common multiple of 4 and 10 is: _____

   Write equivalent fractions with this as the denominator.

   $\frac{3}{4} - \frac{3}{10} =$ _____ − _____

   $=$ _____

2. Subtract. Write the answer in simplest form.

   a) $\frac{5}{8} - \frac{1}{6} =$ _____

   b) $\frac{2}{3} - \frac{5}{12} =$ _____

   c) $\frac{5}{7} - \frac{2}{5} =$ _____

   d) $\frac{2}{5} - \frac{1}{6} =$ _____

3. Complete this magic square so that the sum of every row, column, and diagonal is 1. Write all fractions in simplest form.

$\frac{3}{8}$	$\frac{1}{6}$	
	$\frac{1}{3}$	

HINT
The lowest common multiple of 8, 6, and 3 is 24.

4. Subtract. Regroup if necessary.

a) $4\frac{1}{9} - 2\frac{2}{3} = 4\frac{1}{9} - 2\frac{\quad}{9}$

$= 3\frac{\quad}{9} - \underline{\hspace{2cm}}$

$= \underline{\hspace{2cm}}$

b) $4 - 1\frac{1}{2} = \underline{\hspace{2cm}}$

c) $3\frac{4}{7} - 1\frac{1}{2} = \underline{\hspace{2cm}}$

d) $7\frac{1}{4} - 3\frac{5}{6} = \underline{\hspace{2cm}}$

5. George swam $8\frac{3}{4}$ laps on Monday and $6\frac{1}{5}$ laps on Tuesday.

How many more laps did he swim on Tuesday than on Monday?

_____

6. Amy, Reza, and Jai work together on a group project.
Amy completes $\frac{1}{3}$ of the project.
Reza completes $\frac{1}{4}$ of the project.
What fraction of the project must Jai complete?

HINT
The entire project is 1 whole.

_____

Quick Review

Area models are useful for visualizing multiplication.

➤ The area of a rectangle is length multiplied by width.
A 5 by 3 rectangle covers 15 unit squares.
So, $5 \times 3 = 15$.

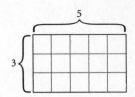

➤ To model $\frac{1}{5} \times \frac{1}{3}$, draw a 5 by 3 rectangle.
The rectangle has 15 equal parts.
A horizontal row of 5 squares represents $\frac{1}{3}$ of the rectangle.
$\frac{1}{5}$ of this row of $\frac{1}{3}$ covers 1 of the 15 parts.
So, $\frac{1}{5} \times \frac{1}{3} = \frac{1}{15}$.

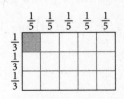

➤ 2 horizontal rows of 5 squares represent $\frac{2}{3}$ of the rectangle.
$\frac{4}{5}$ of these 2 horizontal rows of 5 covers 8 of the 15 parts.
So, $\frac{4}{5} \times \frac{2}{3} = \frac{8}{15}$.

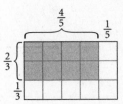

Practice

1. Write the multiplication sentence modelled by the shaded region in each rectangle.

a)

b)

Tip
*Write all fractions
in simplest form.*

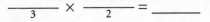
$$\frac{\quad}{3} \times \frac{\quad}{2} = \underline{\quad\quad}$$

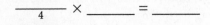
$$\frac{\quad}{4} \times \underline{\quad\quad} = \underline{\quad\quad}$$

c)

d)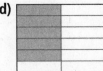

_____   _____

2. Draw an area model for each product. Then find the product.
Write all fractions in simplest form.

a) $\frac{1}{4} \times \frac{3}{4} =$ _____

b) $\frac{1}{2} \times \frac{2}{3} =$ _____

3. Tom took $\frac{3}{4}$ of a pie. He could only eat $\frac{1}{2}$ of what he took.
What fraction of the pie did Tom eat?

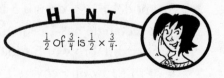
HINT
$\frac{1}{2}$ of $\frac{3}{4}$ is $\frac{1}{2} \times \frac{3}{4}$.

_____

4. Use the area model at the right to calculate each product.

$\frac{1}{5} \times \frac{1}{4} =$ _____

$\frac{2}{5} \times \frac{3}{4} =$ _____

$\frac{3}{5} \times \frac{1}{4} =$ _____

$\frac{1}{5} \times \frac{1}{2} =$ _____

$\frac{3}{5} \times \frac{1}{2} =$ _____

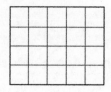

Look for a pattern in the numbers. Describe a relation between the numerator and
denominator of each answer fraction and those of the fractions being multiplied.

_____

_____

_____

_____

_____

Quick Review

➤ To multiply fractions without using a model, multiply the numerators and multiply the denominators.

$$\frac{2}{3} \times \frac{4}{5} = \frac{2 \times 4}{3 \times 5}$$

$$= \frac{8}{15}$$

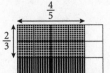

➤ If the numerators and denominators have common factors, divide by these factors before multiplying.

$$\frac{2}{3} \times \frac{9}{10} = \frac{\overset{1}{\cancel{2}} \times \overset{3}{\cancel{9}}}{\underset{1}{\cancel{3}} \times \underset{5}{\cancel{10}}}$$

$$= \frac{1 \times 3}{1 \times 5}$$

$$= \frac{3}{5}$$

$2 \div 2 = 1$	$9 \div 3 = 3$
$3 \div 3 = 1$	$10 \div 2 = 5$

> **Tip**
> The answer will be in simplest form if you divide by the common factors before you multiply the fractions.

➤ Multiply mixed numbers by changing them to improper fractions first.

$$2\frac{1}{5} \times 1\frac{1}{2} = \frac{11}{5} \times \frac{3}{2}$$

$$= \frac{33}{10}$$

$$= \frac{30}{10} + \frac{3}{10}$$

$$= 3\frac{3}{10}$$

> **Tip**
> The question involves mixed numbers. So, give the answer as a mixed number.

Practice

1. Complete this multiplication table. The first one is done for you.

×	$\frac{3}{2}$	$\frac{1}{5}$	$\frac{5}{7}$	$\frac{3}{4}$	$\frac{7}{8}$
$\frac{3}{4}$	$\frac{3 \times 3}{4 \times 2} = \frac{9}{8}$				

2. Match each multiplication to the product.

$\frac{5}{6} \times \frac{2}{7}$ $\frac{1}{4}$

$\frac{3}{2} \times \frac{1}{6}$ $\frac{1}{6}$

$\frac{8}{9} \times \frac{9}{8}$ $\frac{5}{21}$

$\frac{3}{4} \times \frac{2}{9}$ $\frac{6}{35}$

$\frac{9}{10} \times \frac{5}{6}$ 1

$\frac{9}{14} \times \frac{4}{15}$ $\frac{3}{4}$

HINT

Divide the numerator and denominator by common factors before multiplying.

3. Follow each arrow and multiply to complete this chart.

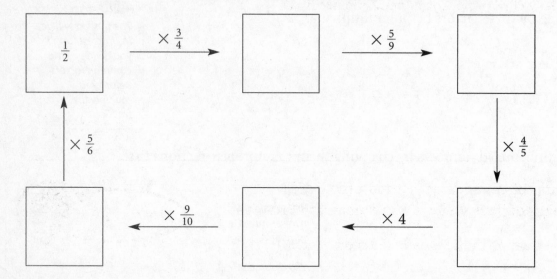

4. Calculate to find each product.

a) $4\frac{4}{5} \times 3\frac{1}{3} = \frac{24}{5} \times$ _____

= _____

b) $1\frac{1}{4} \times 3\frac{2}{5} =$ _____

5. Find a pair of fractions that has each product.

a) 6

b) $\frac{1}{2}$

_____   _____

6. Show that $3\frac{1}{2}$ and $1\frac{2}{5}$ have the same sum and product.

7. A recipe calls for $1\frac{5}{8}$ cups of popcorn. Katie is making $4\frac{1}{2}$ times the recipe. How many cups of popcorn does Katie need?

8. Five-sixths of a class participated in a fundraiser. Two-thirds of these students raised more than $100 each.

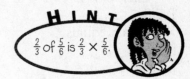

a) What fraction of the class raised more than $100 each?

b) What fraction of the class participated and raised less than $100 each?

Quick Review

Division can be thought of as sharing or grouping.

➤ To divide a whole number by a fraction, use the method of grouping.

To find $2 \div \frac{2}{3}$, think of how many two-thirds are in 2.

Use a number line that shows thirds.

There are 3 groups of two-thirds in 2.

So, $2 \div \frac{2}{3} = 3$.

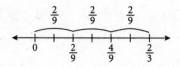

➤ To divide a fraction by a whole number, use the method of sharing.

To find $\frac{2}{3} \div 3$, think of how to divide $\frac{2}{3}$ into 3 equal parts.

Each part is $\frac{1}{3}$ of $\frac{2}{3}$, or $\frac{1}{3} \times \frac{2}{3}$,

which equals $\frac{2}{9}$.

So, $\frac{2}{3} \div 3 = \frac{2}{9}$.

Practice

1. Use this number line to find each quotient.

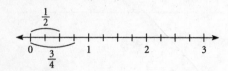

a) $3 \div \frac{1}{2}$

b) $3 \div \frac{3}{4} = $ _____

There are _____ one-halves in 3.

So, $3 \div \frac{1}{2} = $ _____.

2. Use a number line to find each quotient.

a) $4 \div \frac{2}{3} = $ _____

b) $2 \div \frac{2}{5} = $ _____

3. How many $\frac{2}{3}$ cup servings can be poured from 6 cups of juice?

Tip

Use a number line to help you divide.

4. Use a number line to find each quotient.

a) $\frac{3}{4} \div 3$

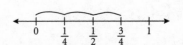

Divide $\frac{3}{4}$ into _____ equal parts.

Each part is $\frac{1}{3}$ of $\frac{3}{4}$.

So, $\frac{3}{4} \div 3 = $ _____.

b) $\frac{3}{5} \div 2 = $ _____

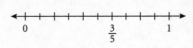

5. Use a number line to divide.

a) $\frac{6}{7} \div 3 = $ _____

b) $\frac{5}{3} \div 2 = $ _____

6. Four children share $\frac{2}{3}$ of a pie. What fraction of the pie does each child get?

Quick Review

$\frac{3}{2} \div \frac{3}{4} = 2$ because there are 2 groups of $\frac{3}{4}$ in $\frac{3}{2}$.

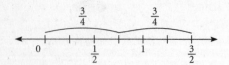

To find $\frac{3}{2} \div \frac{3}{4}$ without using a model, you can use either of these methods:

➤ Write equivalent fractions using a common denominator. Then divide the numerators.

$$\frac{3}{2} \div \frac{3}{4} = \frac{6}{4} \div \frac{3}{4}$$

Because the number of groups of $\frac{3}{4}$ in $\frac{6}{4}$ is the same as the number of groups of 3 in 6, you can simply divide the numerators: $6 \div 3 = 2$

So, $\frac{3}{2} \div \frac{3}{4} = 2$.

➤ Change the division to a multiplication by the **reciprocal**.

$$\frac{3}{2} \div \frac{3}{4} = \frac{\cancel{3}^{1}}{\cancel{2}_{1}} \times \frac{\cancel{4}^{2}}{\cancel{3}_{1}}$$

$$= 2$$

HINT

Dividing by $\frac{3}{4}$ is the same as multiplying by its reciprocal $\frac{4}{3}$.

Practice

1. Divide by finding a common denominator.

a) $\frac{1}{2} \div \frac{1}{6} = \underline{}_{6}\underline{} \div \frac{1}{6}$

    $= \underline{} \div 1$

    $= \underline{}$

b) $\frac{3}{8} \div \frac{3}{4} = \frac{3}{8} \div \underline{}_{8}\underline{}$

    $= 3 \div \underline{}$

    $= \underline{}$

c) $\frac{3}{4} \div \frac{5}{6} = \underline{}$

d) $\frac{3}{10} \div \frac{3}{4} = \underline{}$

Tip
Write all fractions in simplest form.

84

2. Evaluate.

$1 \div \frac{1}{4} =$ _____ $1 \times 4 =$ _____ $\frac{1}{5} \div \frac{3}{5} =$ _____ $\frac{1}{5} \times \frac{5}{3} =$ _____

$3 \div \frac{1}{2} =$ _____ $3 \times 2 =$ _____ $\frac{7}{3} \div \frac{2}{3} =$ _____ $\frac{7}{3} \times \frac{3}{2} =$ _____

Dividing by a fraction is the same as multiplying by its _____.

3. Divide by multiplying by the reciprocal.

> **Tip**
> *Divide by common factors before multiplying.*

a) $\frac{5}{9} \div \frac{3}{5} = \frac{5}{9} \times$ _____

$=$ _____

b) $\frac{1}{12} \div \frac{1}{2} = \frac{1}{12} \times$ _____

$=$ _____

c) $\frac{1}{4} \div \frac{4}{5} =$ _____

d) $\frac{9}{8} \div \frac{3}{16} =$ _____

4. Follow each arrow and divide to complete this chart.

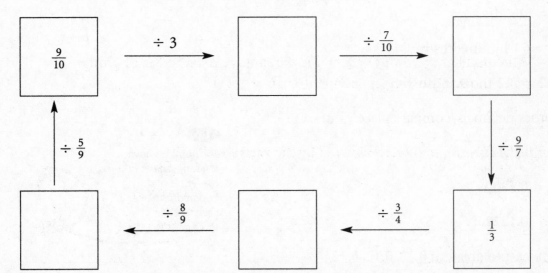

5. Brianna wants to cut a $7\frac{1}{2}$-m long ribbon into $\frac{3}{4}$-m lengths. How many $\frac{3}{4}$-m lengths of ribbon can she cut?

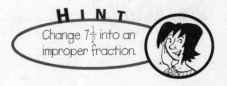

HINT
Change $7\frac{1}{2}$ into an improper fraction.

She can cut _____ lengths of ribbon.

6. Is the quotient of $4 \div \frac{1}{2}$ greater than or less than 4? Explain.

_____

Quick Review

➤ To write a fraction as a decimal, divide the numerator by the denominator.

$\frac{25}{99} = 0.252\ 525\ldots = 0.\overline{25}$ $\frac{25}{100} = 0.25$

$0.\overline{25}$ is a **repeating decimal**. 0.25 is a **terminating decimal**.

It has a bar over the digits that repeat.   It has a definite number of decimal places.

➤ A terminating decimal can be written as fraction.
The number of digits after the decimal point tells the power of 10 in the denominator.

$0.7 = 7$ tenths $= \frac{7}{10}$

$0.71 = 71$ hundredths $= \frac{71}{100}$

$0.712 = 712$ thousandths $= \frac{712}{1000}$

➤ To order decimals, compare place values.

$0.\overline{12} = 0.1212\ldots$

$0.12 = 0.1200$

$0.1\overline{2} = 0.1222\ldots$

From least to greatest: $0.12, 0.1\overline{2}, 0.\overline{12}$

> **Tip**
> The numbers have the same values in the tenths and hundredths places. Compare the thousandths places.

Practice

1. Match each fraction with its corresponding decimal.

$\frac{5}{9}$	$0.1\overline{6}$
$\frac{16}{99}$	$0.\overline{5}$
$\frac{1}{6}$	0.5
$\frac{5}{10}$	$0.\overline{16}$

Which fractions are terminating decimals?

_____

Which fractions are repeating decimals?

_____

2. Complete this table.

Fraction	With Power of 10 as Denominator	Decimal Equivalent
$\frac{3}{5}$	$\frac{6}{10}$	
		0.35
	$\frac{125}{1000}$	
$\frac{12}{25}$		
		0.256
$\frac{9}{50}$		

3. Order each set of decimals from least to greatest.

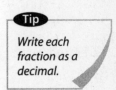

HINT

Compare the tenths place, then the hundredths place, then the thousandths place.

a) $1.\overline{12}$, $1.1\overline{2}$, 1.12, 1.112

$1.\overline{12}$, $= 1.121\ldots$

$1.1\overline{2}$ $= 1.122\ldots$

1.12 $= 1.120$

$1.112 = 1.112$

From least to greatest: _____

b) 0.35, 0.30, 0.53, $0.\overline{35}$

From least to greatest: _____

c) $5\frac{2}{3}$, 5.6, 5.7, $5\frac{4}{7}$

Tip

Write each fraction as a decimal.

From least to greatest: _____

Quick Review

These are the fractional equivalents of 0.1, 0.01, and 0.001:

$$0.1 = \tfrac{1}{10} \qquad\qquad 0.01 = \tfrac{1}{100} \qquad\qquad 0.001 = \tfrac{1}{1000}$$

Dividing by a fraction is the same as multiplying by its reciprocal.

➤ Dividing by 0.1 is the same as multiplying by 10.

   $0.231 \div 0.1 = 0.231 \times 10$ Move the decimal point 1 place to the right.

               $= 2.31$

➤ Dividing by 0.01 is the same as multiplying by 100.

   $0.231 \div 0.01 = 0.231 \times 100$ Move the decimal point 2 places to the right.

               $= 23.1$

➤ Dividing by 0.001 is the same as multiplying by 1000.

   $0.231 \div 0.001 = 0.231 \times 1000$ Move the decimal point 3 places to the right.

               $= 231$

Practice

1. Evaluate and then complete the statements below.

   $1 \div 0.1 =$ _____ $1 \times 10 =$ _____

   $1 \div 0.01 =$ _____ $1 \times 100 =$ _____

   $1 \div 0.001 =$ _____ $1 \times 1000 =$ _____

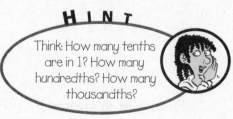

HINT

Think: How many tenths are in 1? How many hundredths? How many thousandths?

Dividing by $\tfrac{1}{10}$ is the same as multiplying by _____.

Dividing by $\tfrac{1}{100}$ is the same as multiplying by _____.

Dividing by $\tfrac{1}{1000}$ is the same as multiplying by _____.

2. Circle the correct answer.

a) $25 \div 0.01$ 　　25　　　　　2.5　　　　　25 000　　　　2500

b) $1.3 \div 0.001$　　0.13　　　　13 000　　　　0.0013　　　　1300

c) $7.0 \div 0.1$　　　700　　　　　70　　　　　0.7　　　　　　7

3. Find the missing number in each division statement.

a) $\frac{?}{10} = 9.4$

9.4×10

$= $ _____

b) $\frac{?}{0.01} = 72$

$72 \times$ _____

$= $ _____

c) $\frac{?}{100} = 0.325$

_____

$= $ _____

d) $\frac{3.8}{?} = 38$

$3.8 \div 38$

$= $ _____

e) $\frac{14.7}{?} = 0.147$

$14.7 \div$ _____

$= $ _____

f) $\frac{6.29}{?} = 6290$

_____

$= $ _____

4. Find each quotient.

a) $4.2 \div 0.7 = 4.2 \div \frac{7}{10}$

$= 4.2 \times$ _____

$= \dfrac{42}{}$

$= $ _____

b) $0.18 \div 0.03 = 0.18 \div \dfrac{3}{}$

$= 0.18 \times \dfrac{}{3}$

$= \dfrac{}{3}$

$= $ _____

> **Tip**
> Change the division by a fraction to a multiplication by its reciprocal.

c) $720 \div 0.008 = $ _____

d) $120 \div 0.4 = $ _____

5. A rectangle is formed by multiplying one side length of a square by 0.3. The length of the rectangle is 0.03 cm. Find the area of the square.

Side length of square: _____

Area of square: _____

In Your Words

Here are some of the important mathematical words of this unit.
Build your own glossary by recording definitions and examples here. The first one is done for you.

lowest common multiple _smallest_
number that is a multiple of 2 or more
numbers
For example, the lowest common multiple
of 5 and 6 is 30.

lowest common denominator

simplest form of a fraction

reciprocal

terminating decimal

repeating decimal

List other mathematical words you need to know.

Unit Review

LESSON

4.1 **1.** Circle the greater fraction in each pair.

a) $\frac{2}{5}, \frac{2}{3}$
b) $\frac{3}{7}, \frac{4}{9}$
c) $\frac{3}{8}, \frac{1}{2}$

2. Order the circled fractions in question 1 from least to greatest. _____

4.2 **3.** Add.

a) $\frac{1}{2} + \frac{2}{5} =$ _____
b) $\frac{1}{2} + \frac{3}{4} + \frac{5}{8} =$ _____
c) $2\frac{2}{3} + 4\frac{5}{12} =$ _____

4. Subtract.

a) $\frac{2}{3} - \frac{1}{6} =$ _____
b) $\frac{5}{8} - \frac{2}{9} =$ _____
c) $2\frac{1}{10} - \frac{4}{5} =$ _____

4.2
4.3 **5.** Maya has $4\frac{1}{2}$ m of ribbon. She uses $1\frac{3}{4}$ m to wrap a present and $\frac{1}{3}$ m to make a bow. How much ribbon is left?

> **Tip**
> Write all fractions with a common denominator.

_____

4.4
4.5 **6.** Multiply. Use an area model if it helps.

a) $4 \times \frac{3}{2} =$ _____
b) $\left(\frac{4}{5}\right)^2 =$ _____
c) $\frac{3}{10} \times \frac{5}{12} =$ _____

4.5 **7.** Pat is 6 years old. Her brother Wayne is $3\frac{1}{3}$ times as old. How old is Wayne?

> **Tip**
> Change mixed numbers to improper fractions before you multiply.

_____

4.4
4.6
8. Write the multiplication or division sentence represented by each model.

a) _____   b) _____

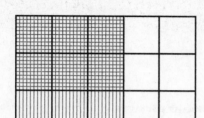
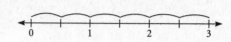

4.6
4.7
9. Divide. Use a number line if it helps.

a) $\frac{3}{2} \div \frac{1}{8} =$ _____   b) $\frac{5}{8} \div 4 =$ _____   c) $\frac{21}{10} \div \frac{27}{5} =$ _____

4.7
10. How many $\frac{3}{4}$ cup servings can you get from $3\frac{1}{2}$ cups of pasta?

_____

4.8
11. Write each fraction as a decimal.

a) $\frac{3}{8} =$ _____   b) $\frac{4}{33} =$ _____

12. Write each decimal as a fraction.

a) 0.2 = _____   b) 0.0001 = _____

c) 0.12 = _____   d) 0.005 = _____

> **Tip**
> Count the number of digits after the decimal point to find the power of 10 in the denominator.

4.9
13. Use mental math to divide.

a) 23.5 ÷ 0.001 = _____   b) 0.468 ÷ 0.2 = _____

c) 1.25 ÷ 0.05 = _____   d) 2.468 ÷ 0.08 = _____

Just for Fun

Crossword Diagram

The word QUALITATIVE is given as a start.
Place these mathematical words in the correct squares to complete the diagram.

BIAS	CENSUS	DATA	FREQUENCY
GRAPH	HISTOGRAM	INFERENCE	MEAN
MEDIAN	MODE	OUTLIER	POPULATION
RANGE	SAMPLE	SURVEY	TREND

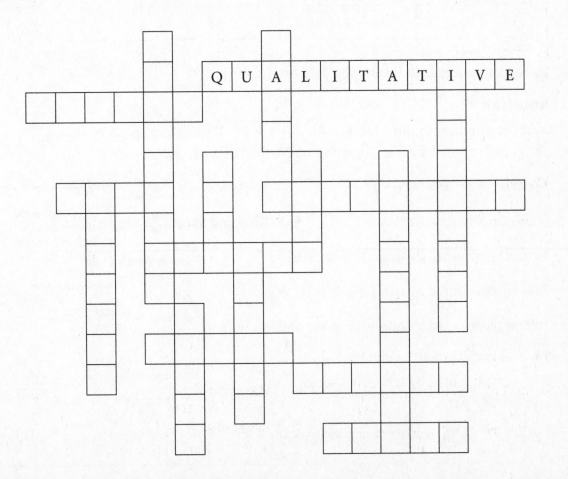

Skills You'll Need

Using a Percent Circle to Draw a Circle Graph

A percent circle has 10 equal sectors, each representing 10% of the circle.

Each sector is divided into 10 equal parts, each representing 1% of the circle.

The entire circle is 100%.

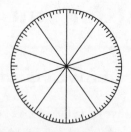

Example 1

Brenna recorded these data about the shoes in her family's closet.

Shoes in Family Closet			
Sandals	**Dress Shoes**	**Slippers**	**Running Shoes**
6	4	3	7

Use a percent circle to display the data on a circle graph.

Solution

Add the numbers in the table: $6 + 4 + 3 + 7 = 20$. There are 20 pairs of shoes. Write each type of shoe as a fraction of 20, then as a percent.

Sandals: $\frac{6}{20} = \frac{30}{100} = 30\%$ Dress Shoes: $\frac{4}{20} = \frac{20}{100} = 20\%$

Slippers: $\frac{3}{20} = \frac{15}{100} = 15\%$ Running Shoes: $\frac{7}{20} = \frac{35}{100} = 35\%$

30% is represented by three 10% sectors.

20% is represented by two 10% sectors.

15% is represented by one 10% sector and five 1% parts.

35% is represented by three 10% sectors and five 1% parts.

Label each sector. Write a title for the graph.

Shoes in Family Closet

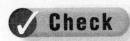

✓ Check

1. Use a percent circle to draw a circle graph for these data.

Students in Class 8B – Favourite Movie Series			
Star Wars	**Lord of the Rings**	**Harry Potter**	**James Bond**
6	7	9	3

There are _____ students in Class 8B.

Star Wars: $\dfrac{}{25} = \dfrac{}{100} =$ _____ %

Lord of the Rings: $\dfrac{}{25} = \dfrac{}{100} =$ _____ %

Harry Potter: $\dfrac{}{25} = \dfrac{}{100} =$ _____ %

James Bond: $\dfrac{}{25} = \dfrac{}{100} =$ _____ %

Favourite Movie Series

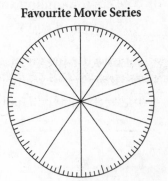

Trends in Graphs

Data and graphs sometimes show a pattern or trend.
When a graph goes up to the right, the value on the vertical axis is increasing.
When a graph goes down to the right, the value on the vertical axis is decreasing.
When a graph is horizontal, the value on the vertical axis is not changing.

Example 2

This line graph represents the height of snow on Jacob's front lawn during one week in March.

a) Describe any trends in the graph.

b) What was the height of snow on Sunday? On Friday? How do you know?

Height of Snow During a Week in March

Solution

a) The first **S** on the horizontal axis represents Sunday. The graph goes up to the right from Sunday to Thursday, so the height of snow was increasing.

Example 2 (continued)

The line segment from Sunday to Monday is steeper than the line segment from Monday to Thursday. This means more snow fell from Sunday to Monday than from Monday to Thursday.

The line segment from Thursday to Friday is horizontal.
This means the height of snow remained the same during these two days.

The line segment from Friday to Saturday goes down to the right.
This means the height of snow was decreasing. The snow was melting.

b) The corresponding value on the vertical axis for Sunday is 10 cm.
The height of snow on Sunday was 10 cm.

To find the height of snow on Friday, draw a vertical line from the **F** on the horizontal axis to meet the graph. From this point, draw a horizontal line to meet the vertical axis. The height of snow was 40 cm on Friday.

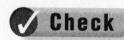

Check

2. Yummy Pizza Parlour added 3 new large combo pizzas to their takeout menu. These line graphs display the number of orders over a 6-week period.

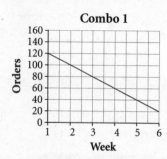 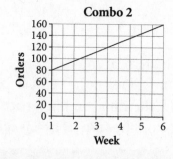 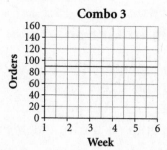

a) Which combo had no change in sales? How do you know?

_____

b) Which combo should be removed from the menu? Explain.

_____

c) Which combo is becoming more popular? How do you know?

_____

d) How many of each type of combo was ordered in the sixth week? How do you know?

_____

_____

Quick Review

➤ In a **census** survey, data are collected from all the people in a **population**. For example, when every student in a school is asked to name her/his favourite movie, this survey on the school's favourite movie is a census survey.

➤ In a **sample** survey, data are collected from a portion or a sample of a population. For example, when only 1 out 5 students in each grade in a school is asked to name her/his favourite movie, this survey on the school's favourite movie is a sample survey. A sample survey is less costly and requires less time than a census survey.

➤ A sample is biased if it does not accurately represent the population. A survey is reliable if the results can be duplicated in another survey. A survey is valid if the results represent the population. For example, when only girls are surveyed to determine the school's favourite movie, the sample is biased and the survey is not valid. This survey will be more reliable when data are collected from an approximately equal numbers of boys and girls.

➤ Data that can be measured using numbers are quantitative data. They are of 2 types: **Discrete** data, such as the number of students, are described using whole numbers. **Continuous** data, such as the length of a room, are measured on a continuum, and can be described using decimals or fractions. Qualitative data are data that cannot be measured using numbers. For example, data collected for the school's favourite movie are qualitative data.

Practice

1. A survey is conducted with data collected by each method listed. Classify the survey as a census or a sample survey. One is done for you.

   a) To find the favourite book of Grade 8 students in a school, every Grade 8 student in the school is surveyed.   _____census_____

   b) To check the quality of food provided by the school cafeteria, some students in each class are asked to give their opinion.   _____

   c) To find the favourite music group of teenagers of a city, twenty 16-year-olds in each school of the city are surveyed.   _____

   d) To find the favourite item on a restaurant's menu, all customers eating in the restaurant are surveyed.   _____

2. State if data collected for each survey topic are *discrete*, *continuous*, or *qualitative*. One is done for you.

a) height of a bean plant from seed   _continuous_

b) favourite musical instrument of Grade 8 students   _____

c) number of students on each school bus   _____

d) temperature of boiled water as it cools   _____

3. Identify the population for which data are to be collected.

a) The hotel management wants to know how many of their guests use the spa facilities.

_____

b) The school principal wants to know how many teachers need a computer at their desk.

_____

c) A lawn-care company wants to know if their customers prefer environmentally friendly products for their lawn.

_____

4. Is each sample biased or reliable? Justify your answer.

a) To determine if more parks should be built, a survey of all families who have children under 12 is conducted.

_____

_____

_____

HINT

Think: Does the sample represent the population?

b) To find out if students want more school dances, one in three students is randomly selected from each grade for the survey.

_____

_____

c) To find out if teenagers preferred skiing over snowboarding, all teenagers enrolled in snowboarding lessons were surveyed.

_____

_____

5. For each situation below:

- Explain why the sampling method might provide biased data.

- Describe how the sampling method can be changed so the data collected represent the population.

a) The prom committee wants to know if students prefer a buffet dinner to a served dinner. The committee surveys the first 10 students that buy prom tickets to find out.

_____

_____

_____

_____

> **Tip**
> *Think: Would 10 students be enough to represent the population?*

b) The administrator of a fitness centre wants to find out if the centre should extend its hours of operation. People who use the centre between 8 a.m. and 12 noon on weekdays are surveyed.

_____

_____

_____

_____

6. For each situation, would you suggest a sample survey or a census survey be conducted? Explain.

a) A car manufacturer wants to find out if Canadian families with young children prefer a minivan to an SUV as the family car.

_____

_____

_____

b) A district school board wants to know how many students who are in the Grade 10 math course achieve scores over 90%.

_____

_____

_____

Quick Review

➤ Data and graphs may be used to make convincing arguments.
Some arguments are more convincing than others.

For example, Lucas and Tia made 2 different arguments using the data in this table.

Amount of Time Spent with Friends after School (to nearest minute)						
	< 30 min	30–59 min	60–89 min	90–119 min	≥120 min	Total
Girls	6	10	15	15	4	50
Boys	3	9	16	17	5	50
Total	9	19	31	32	9	100

Lucas added the data in columns 4 and 5 to find that 22 boys and 19 girls spent more than 90 min with their friends after school. He used this to argue that boys spend more time with their friends than girls do.

Tia added the totals of columns 3 and 4 to find that 63 boys and girls spend 60–120 min with their friends after school. She used this to argue that over 60% of boys and girls spend 1–2 h with their friends after school.

Tia's argument is more convincing than Lucas' because only 3 more boys than girls spend more than 90 min with their friends after school. The numbers are too close for Lucas' argument to be convincing.

➤ Sometimes, a graph shows a trend or relationship in the data. When you use data to predict a value in the future, or to estimate a value between given data, you make an **inference**. When you use data to make a conclusion, you infer.

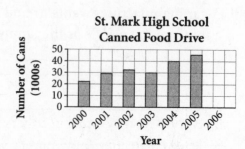

St. Mark High School
Canned Food Drive

For example, using the data from this graph, you can make valid arguments and inferences.

The graph shows that, other than 2003, the height of the bar for each year is higher than the previous year. A convincing argument would be that St. Mark High School is collecting more cans from year to year.

You can also infer that, if this trend continues, the number of cans collected in 2006 will be greater than the number collected in 2005. The prediction, or inference, you can make is that over 50 000 cans will be collected in 2006.

Practice

1. a) What does the graph show?

_____

_____

_____

_____

_____

Attendance at Movie Theatre

b) What inferences can you make from the graph? Explain.

_____

_____

_____

_____

_____

> **Tip**
> Compare the heights of the bars for adults and youths for each day.

c) How can the graph be used to justify each argument?

  i) Saturday is the most popular day for people to go to the movies.

  _____

  _____

  _____

  _____

> **Tip**
> Add the heights of the bars for adults and youths for each day.

  ii) Approximately equal numbers of adults and youths go the movies on Friday, Saturday, and Sunday.

  _____

  _____

  _____

  _____

> **Tip**
> Add the heights of the bars for the 3 days for adults and for youths.

101

2. Tawanda recorded in this table the type of cars driven by people in his neighbourhood.

Type of Car	Van	SUV	Sports Car	Sedan
Number	23	14	5	9

He used the data in the table to make this argument:
"Most people in my neighbourhood drive a van."

a) Is Tawanda's argument valid? Explain.

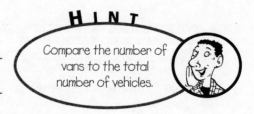

HINT

Compare the number of vans to the total number of vehicles.

_____

_____

_____

b) Write two convincing arguments that could be justified by the data in the table.

_____

_____

_____

3. a) What does this graph show?

_____

_____

_____

_____

_____

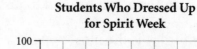

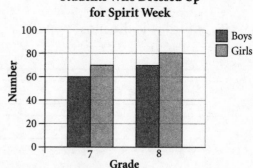

b) Below are 3 arguments made by members of the Student Council.
A: Boys have less school spirit than girls.
B: Grade 8 students have more school spirit than Grade 7 students.
C: Grade 7 students have more school spirit than Grade 8 students.

If there are about the same number of students in each grade, which argument do you think is most valid? Justify your answer.

_____

_____

_____

c) The data in this table shows the actual number of boys and girls in Grades 7 and 8.

	Grade 7	Grade 8	Total
Boys	62	78	142
Girls	71	92	168
Total	133	170	310

H I N T

Think about those who did not dress up.

With this new information, which argument in part b is most valid? Explain.

_____

_____

_____

_____

_____

_____

4. a) What relationship does this graph show?

_____

_____

_____

_____

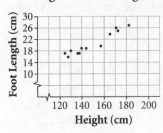

Height vs. Foot Length

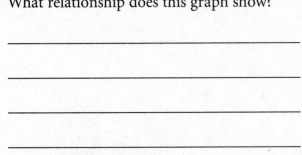

b) What inferences can you make from this graph? Explain.

_____

_____

_____

c) How can you use the graph to estimate the foot length of a person who is 140 cm tall?

_____

_____

_____

Quick Review

Some graphs are more suitable than others for displaying certain data.
You can use a graph to identify trends and make inferences.

➤ A circle graph displays data that are parts of one whole.

Shoes in Family Closet

➤ A line graph displays data that changes over time.

Height of Snow During a Week in March

➤ A bar graph displays data that can be counted. When there are 2 sets of data, a double-bar graph is used.

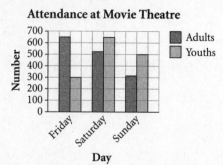

Attendance at Movie Theatre

➤ A scatter plot displays two related sets of data that are measured or counted.

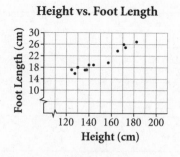

Height vs. Foot Length

Sometimes a graph can misrepresent data because of the way it is drawn.

These two graphs display the same data. The left graph gives the impression that the antique car value is increasing dramatically because the vertical scale does not begin at 0. The right graph is a more accurate representation because the vertical scale begins at 0.

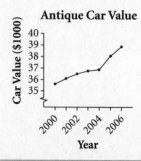

Antique Car Value

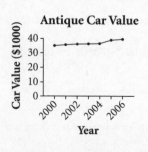

Antique Car Value

1. This table displays the number of students enrolled in driver's education at a high school from 1995 to 2005.

a) How many more students enrolled in driver's education in 2005 than in 1995?

_____

_____

_____

Students Enrolled in Driver's Education		
Year	Females	Males
1995	23	42
1996	27	46
1997	32	51
1998	34	57
1999	38	63
2000	45	72
2001	56	83
2002	67	98
2003	84	107
2004	95	118
2005	113	129

b) What types of graphs could be used to display the data? Explain.

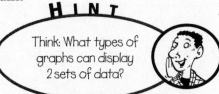

HINT

Think: What types of graphs can display 2 sets of data?

_____

_____

_____

c) Display the data using the most appropriate graph. Justify your choice.

_____

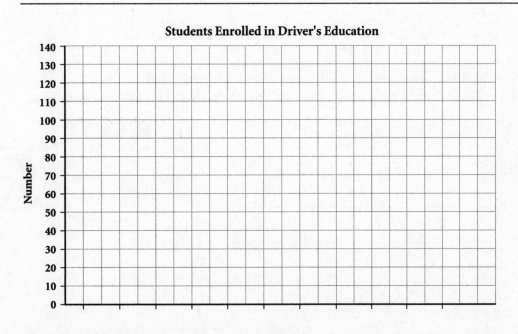

Students Enrolled in Driver's Education

2. Use the data table and the graph you have drawn in question 1 for the number of students enrolled in driver's education at a high school from 1995 to 2005.

a) What trends do you see in the data?

Tip

Look for trends in the numbers in the table.

_____

_____

_____

_____

_____

b) How does the graph show the trends?

Tip

Use the graph to find how the values on the vertical axis change with time. Also, make comparisons between females and males.

_____

_____

_____

_____

_____

c) Predict the enrollment for males in 2008. Justify your answer.

_____

_____

_____

_____

d) Adreece examined the data in the table and made this argument:
"Males are better drivers than females because more males are in driver's education."

Is this a valid argument? Explain.

H I N T

Think: Do the enrollment numbers tell you who is a better driver?

_____

_____

_____

_____

3. a) What does the data in this table represent?

_____

_____

_____

b) Display the data using a suitable graph. Justify your choice.

_____

_____

Average Marks on Math Topics		
Topic	**Girls**	**Boys**
Number	65%	60%
Algebra	72%	65%
Geometry	80%	77%
Measurement	80%	84%
Probability	70%	75%

Average Marks on Math Topics

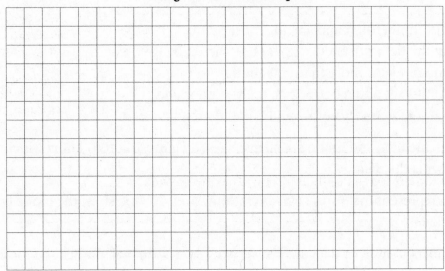

c) Redraw the graph to give the impression that girls are much better in Number and in Algebra than boys.

Average Marks on Math Topics

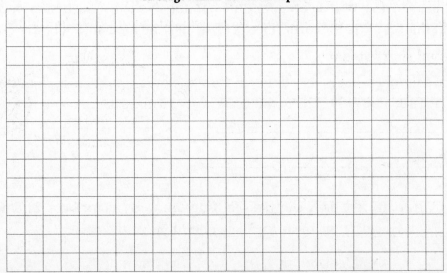

> **Tip**
> _Change the vertical scale to emphasize the difference between the marks for girls and boys._

Quick Review

➤ For a set of data, the measures of central tendency are: mean, median, and mode.

The mean is the sum of data values divided by the number of data values.

The median is the middle number when the numbers are arranged in order.
If there is an even number of data, the median is the mean of the 2 middle numbers.
For example, in this set of data: 7, **12**, **18**, 21, the median is the mean of the 2 middle numbers 12 and 18.

Median = $\frac{12+18}{2}$ = 15

The mode is the number that appears the most often.
For example, in this set of data: 8, 2, 7, **9**, 11, **9**, the mode is 9.
There may be no mode or more than one mode.
For example, in this set of data: 3, 6, 2, 9, there is no mode.
In this set of data: **4**, <u>5</u>, 3, **4**, <u>5</u>, both 4 and 5 are modes.

➤ Since the mean, median, and mode are all averages, it is important to know which one best represents the data.

When the data represent measures such as clothing sizes or shoe sizes, the mode best represents the data.

When the numbers in a set of data are not very different from each other, the mean is the best average. For example, the mean is used to represent the average of this set of math scores: 76, 78, 79, 69, 81

Mean = $\frac{76+78+79+69+81}{5}$ = $\frac{383}{5}$ = 76.6

When the numbers in a set of data are very different, the median is the best average.
For example, in this set of math scores: 45, 67, **75**, 87, 98, the median, 75, best represents the set of data.

➤ In a set of data, a number that is very different from the other numbers is an **outlier**.
In this set of data: **10**, 35, 37, 39, 42, **78**, the outliers are 10 and 78.

Practice

1. During one week in February, the daily snowfalls in Kingston were: 5 cm, 4 cm, 21 cm, 6 cm, 3 cm, 7 cm, 3 cm. Calculate the mean, median, and mode of the data.

Mean: _____   Median: _____   Mode: _____

2. Use the data in question 1. Calculate the mean, median, and mode without the outlier.

Data without the outlier: _____

Tip
The outlier is very different from the other numbers.

Mean: _____ Median: _____ Mode: _____

3. The mode of the sizes of jeans sold in the store last week was medium. Explain what this means.

_____

_____

4. Sophie has these scores on her math quizzes: 55, 89, 78, 99, 85, 83, 82, 87, 80, 78
For the mid-term report, Sophie could choose between using the highest average of all 10 quiz scores or the highest average of those scores without the outliers.
What should Sophie's choice be? Justify your answer.

For all 10 scores:

Mean = _____ = _____

Arrange the 10 scores in order: _____

Median = _____ = _____   Mode = _____

The scores without the outliers are: _____

Mean = _____ = _____

Median = _____ = _____   Mode = _____

_____

_____

5. To be on the 1-km race team, Celia must have a mean time less than 5 min 50 s in 6 tryout races. Her times in 5 races are: 6 min 2 s, 5 min 53 s, 5 min 45 s, 6 min, and 5 min 34 s. What time should Celia aim for in her sixth race to make the team?

Time that Celia has to aim for in the 6th tryout race: _____

Is this possible? Explain. _____

_____

6. The heights of the girls in Class 8A and 8B are recorded in these 2 stem-and-leaf plots.

Class 8A Girls' Height (cm)

Stem	Leaf
11	
12	1
13	4 4 5 7 9
14	2 4 7 9 9 9
15	4 4 5 7 8
16	9
17	5
18	6

Class 8B Girls' Height (cm)

Stem	Leaf
11	8
12	3
13	2 8 9
14	0 1 3 5 5 8
15	0 1 2 4 8 8 8
16	
17	8
18	7

a) What are the outliers in the data for the heights of each class?

8A: _____

8B: _____

b) Without the outliers, determine the mean, median, and mode height of the 2 classes.

8A: Mean = _____   Median = _____   Mode = _____

8B: Mean = _____   Median = _____   Mode = _____

c) With the outliers, the average heights for the 2 classes are:
8A: Mean = 149.4 cm   Median = 149 cm   Mode = 149 cm
8B: Mean = 147.9 cm   Median = 146.5 cm   Mode = 158 cm
Compare the average heights of the 2 classes with and without the outliers.
What do you notice? Explain.

_____

_____

_____

_____

Quick Review

➤ A bar graph is used to compare items that are measured or counted. The bars are separated by a space. The length or height of each bar represents a number.

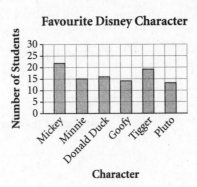

➤ For a large amount of data that can be arranged in numerical order and grouped, a **histogram** is used to display the data.

➤ Adam collected data on the number of minutes Grade 8 students spent listening to music each day. He rounded each data value to the nearest minute.

To draw a histogram, Adam arranged the data in numerical order and grouped them into equal intervals as shown in this table. Each data value belongs exactly to 1 interval. The number of pieces of data in that interval is the frequency.

Adam used the horizontal axis to represent the time intervals in minutes, and the vertical axis to represent the number of pieces of data, or frequency. The height of each bar represents the frequency of that interval. Since the data are continuous, there is no space between the bars.

Time Spent Listening to Music	
Time (min per day)	Number of Students
0–9	1
10–19	6
20–29	12
30–39	15
40–49	21
50–59	16
60–69	13
70–79	6
80–89	2
90–99	3

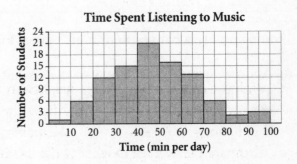

1. Draw an appropriate graph to display the data on the frequency of jewellery purchased within each price interval (rounded to nearest dollar). Explain your choice of graph.

Price ($)	0–4	5–9	10–14	15–19	20–24	25–29	30–34	35–39	40–44	45–49
Frequency	28	23	27	19	14	12	8	5	3	1

Frequency of Jewellery Purchased

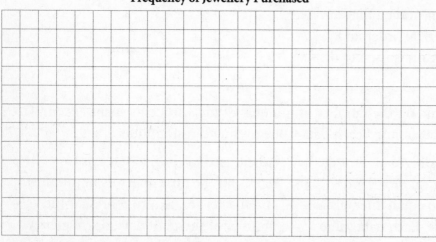

Write 2 inferences you can make from the graph. Explain.

_____

_____

_____

2. Would you use a bar graph or a histogram to display each set of data? Explain.

a) Andrew recorded the length, to the nearest minute, of 25 movies.
152, 165, 189, 126, 138, 119, 127, 136, 155, 129, 138, 130,
140, 168, 172, 166, 147, 152, 129, 133, 148, 152, 160, 157

Think: Can the data be grouped?

_____

_____

b) David recorded the number of each type of shell he found on the beach.
starfish: 4; conk: 7; snail: 12, clam: 35; silver dollar: 10; other: 3

_____

3. To order new uniforms for the school junior and senior football teams, Jari recorded the waist size, to the nearest centimetre, of each member. Here are the results.

78, 112, 85, 72, 90, 99, 84, 75, 101, 67, 83, 99, 80, 105, 82, 88, 74, 93, 79, 80, 78, 86, 95, 81, 92, 100, 85, 79, 90, 88, 94, 103, 76, 89, 70, 89, 96, 98, 76, 74, 83, 92, 90, 106, 115, 84, 81, 95, 97, 87, 76, 88, 69, 90, 92

a) Display the data in a stem-and-leaf plot.

b) What is the range of the data?

_____

c) What is a suitable interval to show this range of data?

_____

_____

d) Use the stem-and-leaf plot to make a frequency table.

e) What can you tell from the stem-and-leaf plot that you cannot tell from the frequency table?

_____

_____

_____

f) Use the frequency table to draw a histogram.

g) What can you infer about the football players?

_____

_____

_____

_____

_____

Waist Size of Football Players

Stem	Leaf

Interval	Frequency

Waist Size of Football Players

Quick Review

➤ A circle graph is used to graph data that represent parts of one whole.
Each piece of data is written as a fraction of the whole.
To find the angle of a sector in a circle graph that represents the piece of data, multiply the fraction by 360°.
To find the percent of the circle that represents the piece of data, multiply the fraction by 100%.

➤ This table shows the choice of a drink for lunch of all students in Class 8C.

Type of Drink	Milk	Juice	Pop	Chocolate Milk
Number of Students	9	7	6	2

To draw a circle graph to display the data, follow these steps:

There are 24 students in the class. Write a fraction out of 24 for each type of drink.

Milk: $\frac{9}{24}$; juice: $\frac{7}{24}$; pop: $\frac{6}{24}$; chocolate milk: $\frac{2}{24}$

Find each sector angle. Multiply each fraction by 360°.
Then find each percent. Multiply each fraction by 100%.

Milk: $\frac{9}{24} \times 360° = 135°$; $\frac{9}{24} \times 100\% \doteq 38\%$

Juice: $\frac{7}{24} \times 360° = 105°$; $\frac{7}{24} \times 100\% \doteq 29\%$

Pop: $\frac{6}{24} \times 360° = 90°$; $\frac{6}{24} \times 100\% = 25\%$

Chocolate milk: $\frac{2}{24} \times 360° = 30°$; $\frac{2}{24} \times 100\% \doteq 8\%$

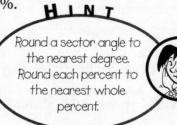

H I N T

Round a sector angle to the nearest degree. Round each percent to the nearest whole percent.

Draw a large circle and draw one radius.
Use a protractor to measure the greatest sector angle, 135°.
Draw another radius to make a sector with this angle.
Continue to make a sector for each angle.
Label each sector with its percent.

Choices of Drink for Lunch

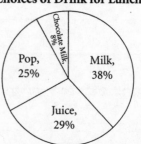

Practice

1. This table shows the sales of muffins during one Saturday morning at Muffin House.

   a) The sales of different muffins on that morning will be displayed in a circle graph. Complete the table for each type of muffin sold.

Type of Muffin	Number of Muffins	Sector Angle	Percent
Blueberry	12	$\frac{12}{55} \times 360° \doteq 79°$	$\frac{12}{55} \times 100\% \doteq 22\%$
Chocolate Chip	5	$\frac{}{55} \times 360° \doteq$ _____ °	_____ $\times 100\% \doteq$ _____ %
Apple Bran	8	_____ $\times 360° \doteq$ _____ °	_____ $\times 100\% \doteq$ _____ %
Cranberry	14	_____ $\times 360° \doteq$ _____ °	_____ $\times 100\% \doteq$ _____ %
Carrot	6	_____ $\times 360° \doteq$ _____ °	_____ $\times 100\% \doteq$ _____ %
Very Berry	10	_____ $\times 360° \doteq$ _____ °	_____ $\times 100\% \doteq$ _____ %
Total	55	360°	100%

   b) Use your results from part a to draw a circle graph.

Sales of Muffins

> **Tip**
> To make a sector, draw a radius, measure the angle with a protractor, and draw another radius.

   c) What inferences can you make from this circle graph?

   _____

   _____

   _____

2. A high school has a budget of $18 000 to buy textbooks for new courses.
This table shows the number of students taking new courses in each department.

a) The number of students taking new courses in each department will be displayed in a circle graph. Complete the table for each department.

Department	Number of Students	Sector Angle	Percent
Math	165	_____ × 360° ≐ _____°	_____ × 100% ≐ _____ %
Science	84	_____ × 360° = _____°	_____ × 100% ≐ _____ %
English	120	_____ × 360° = _____°	_____ × 100% = _____ %
Computer	63	_____ × 360° ≐ _____°	_____ × 100% ≐ _____ %
Business	48	_____ × 360° = _____°	_____ × 100% = _____ %
Total	_____	360°	100%

b) Use your results from part a to draw a circle graph.

c) From the circle graph, which two departments have the most students taking new courses?

_____

_____

d) How much money should be given to each of these two departments? Explain.

Students Taking New Courses

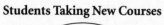

H I N T

Multiply $18 000 by the percent for each department.

_____

_____

In Your Words

Here are some of the important mathematical words of this unit.
Build your own glossary by recording definitions and examples here. The first one is done for you.

outlier _a number in a set of data that is much greater or much smaller than other values in the same set For example, the outliers in this set of data 2, 11, 14, 16, 18, 27 are 2 and 27._

population of a survey

census

sample survey

inference

histogram

List other mathematical words you need to know.

Unit Review

LESSON

5.1 **1.** The Ontario Ministry of Education wants to find out if parents prefer 2 weeks off to 1 week off at March break.
Would you suggest a sample survey or a census survey be conducted? Explain.

_____

_____

2. To find out if customers are happy with the store hours, the Independent Grocer randomly surveyed 500 customers who bought groceries for one week.
Is this sample biased or reliable? Justify your answer.

_____

_____

_____

> **Tip**
> *Think: Is the sample size large enough to represent the population?*

5.2 **3.** Justin recorded in this table the favourite type of food that his classmates enjoyed eating.

Type of Food	Italian	Greek	Chinese	Canadian	Mexican
Number	6	4	10	3	7

He used the data in the table to make this argument:
"Most students in my class prefer Chinese food to other types of food."

a) Is Justin's argument valid? Explain.

_____

_____

b) Write two convincing arguments that could be justified by the data in the table.

_____

_____

5.3
5.4 **4.** The data in this table represent Ari's and Mila's monthly earnings from July to December.

Month	Jul	Aug	Sep	Oct	Nov	Dec
Ari	$2600	$2260	$2200	$1980	$1820	$1630
Mila	$1850	$1925	$2025	$2150	$2325	$2400

a) Display the data using a suitable graph.
Justify your choice.

_____

_____

_____

H I N T

Think: What types of
graphs can display
2 sets of data?

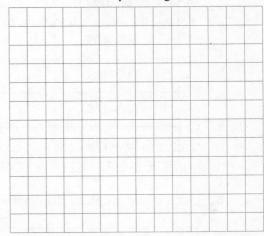

Monthly Earnings ($)

b) What trends do you see in the data? Explain.

_____

_____

_____

_____

_____

c) Find the mean monthly earnings for Ari in the 6 months.

_____

d) Find the mean monthly earnings for Ari without the outlier.
Explain how the mean is affected by the outlier.

_____

5.4
5.5

5. This stem-and-leaf plot shows the number of nickels collected by each class for the school
charity fund.

Nickels Collected by Each Class

Stem	Leaf
8	0 1 2 3 4 5 5 6 6 8 8 9 9
9	0 0 2 2 2 2 3 4 5 5 6 7 8 9
10	0 5 6 7 8 9
11	0 1 1 3 5 8
12	2 6 7
13	9

a) Find the median and mode number of nickels.

Median: _____ Mode: _____

b) What are the outliers? _____
How do they affect the median and mode?

_____

_____

c) Use the stem-and-leaf plot to make a frequency table. Then draw a histogram.

Interval	Frequency
80–89	
90–99	
100–109	
110–119	
120–129	
130–139	

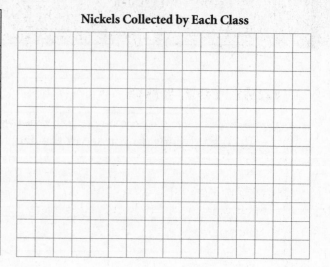

Nickels Collected by Each Class

5.6 **6.** Use a circle graph to display the data in this table.

Car Colour Preferred by Grade 8 Students						
Colour	Red	Yellow	Silver	Black	Blue	Other
Number of Students	12	2	3	11	5	2

> **Tip**
> Write parts of a whole as fractions. To find the sector angle, multiply the fraction by 360°.

Colour	Sector Angle	Percent
Total	**360°**	**100%**

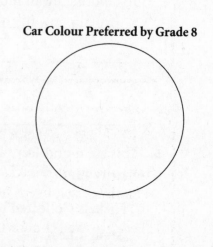

Car Colour Preferred by Grade 8

Explain why a circle graph is preferred to other types of graphs for displaying the data.

_____

_____

UNIT 6 Circles

Just for Fun

Handshakes

People are standing in a circle.
Each person shakes hands with every
other person in the circle.

Draw a circle.
Then draw dots to represent the people.
Join any 2 dots to represent a handshake.

Record your results in the table.

Write a pattern for the number of handshakes.

Number of People	Number of Handshakes
1	0
2	1
3	3
4	
5	
6	
7	

_____

_____

Win the Chocolate

A Game for 4 or more

Everyone sits in a circle. One person is given a brown button.
Set a timer that beeps in 1 minute.

These are the rules for the game:
The button is passed around the circle in a clockwise direction.
When the timer beeps and the button is with you, you are out of the game.
Place the button on the floor in front of you.

The next person in the circle picks up the button and the game continues.
The last person in the game wins the chocolate.

Skills You'll Need

Rounding Measurements

When a number is rounded to a certain number of decimal places,
look at the digit to the right of the decimal place to which you are rounding.

- If this digit is less than 5, round down.
  That is, you drop this and all other digits to its right.
- If this digit is 5 or greater, round up.
  That is, you drop this and all other digits to its right, and add 1 to the digit to its left.

Since 0.1 cm = 1 mm, rounding a measurement in centimetres to millimetres is the same as rounding to 1 decimal place.

Since 0.01 m = 1 cm, rounding a measurement in metres to centimetres is the same as rounding to 2 decimal places.

Example

a) Round 23.76 cm to the nearest millimetre.

b) Round 1.3829 m to the nearest centimetre.

Solution

a) Rounding 23.76 cm to the nearest millimetre is the same as rounding to 1 decimal place. Look at the digit to the right of 7, which is 6.
   Since 6 > 5, round up. 7 becomes 8.
   So, 23.76 cm is 23.8 cm to the nearest millimetre.

b) Rounding 1.3829 m to the nearest centimetre is the same as rounding to 2 decimal places. Look at the digit to the right of 8, which is 2.
   Since 2 < 5, round down. Drop 2 and all digits to its right.
   So, 1.3829 m is 1.38 m to the nearest centimetre.

✓ Check

1. Round to the nearest centimetre.

a) 2.467 m = _____   b) 40.912 m = _____   c) 58.89 cm = _____

2. Round to the nearest millimetre.

a) 2.467 m = _____   b) 40.9127 m = _____   c) 58.19 cm = _____

Quick Review

➤ A circle is a closed curve. All points on the circle are the same distance from the centre of the circle.

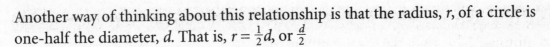

The distance between a point on a circle and the centre of the circle is a **radius** of the circle. The plural of radius is radii.

The distance between two points on a circle through its centre is a **diameter** of the circle.

➤ The length of any diameter, d, of a circle is two times the length of any radius, r.
That is, $d = 2r$

Another way of thinking about this relationship is that the radius, r, of a circle is one-half the diameter, d. That is, $r = \frac{1}{2}d$, or $\frac{d}{2}$

You can find the diameter of a circle for a given radius, and vice versa.

For example, in a circle, $d = 10$.
Since $r = \frac{1}{2}d$, $r = 5$.
If $r = 5$ is given, then use $d = 2r$.
$d = 2 \times 5 = 10$

Practice

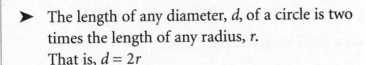

1. This circle has the centre at point O.

   a) Draw a radius of the circle.

   What is the radius of the circle? _____

   b) Draw a diameter of the circle.

   What is the diameter of the circle? _____

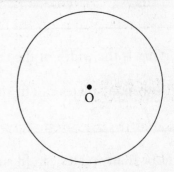

2. From your results in question 1, write a relationship between the radius and the diameter of a circle.

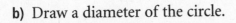

3. Find the diameter of the circle with each radius.

a) 12 cm _____

b) 27 cm _____

c) 3.4 cm _____

d) 1.23 m _____

e) $\frac{1}{3}$ m _____

f) $\frac{7}{10}$ cm _____

4. Find the radius of the circle with each diameter.

a) 12 cm _____

b) 27 cm _____

c) 3.4 cm _____

d) 1.23 m _____

e) $\frac{1}{3}$ m _____

f) $\frac{7}{10}$ cm _____

5. Write the steps you would take to draw a circle with diameter 4 cm.

6. Circular plates with diameter 12 cm are placed side by side on the top of a table. The table measures 2.4 m by 1.2 m.

> **Tip**
> To convert metres to centimetres, multiply by 100.

a) What is the length of the tabletop in centimetres? _____

b) How many plates can fit side by side along the length of the table?

_____

c) What is the width of the tabletop in centimetres? _____

d) How many plates can fit side by side along the width of the table?

_____

e) How many plates can fit side by side on the tabletop with no part of a plate extending over the edge of the table?

_____

Quick Review

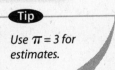

➤ The distance around a circle is its **circumference**.

The ratio of the circumference, C, to the diameter, d, of a circle, $\frac{C}{d}$, is a constant close to 3.

That is, the circumference is approximately 3 times the diameter, or 6 times the radius.

➤ The Greek letter π is used to represent the constant for $\frac{C}{d}$.

In symbols: $\frac{C}{d} = \pi$
π is an **irrational number** equal to about 3.14.

> **HINT**
> An irrational number is a decimal that never repeats and never terminates.

So, the circumference, C, is π multiplied by d.

$C = \pi d$

Since $d = 2r$, $C = \pi \times 2r$, or $C = 2\pi r$

➤ You can use one of the formulas above to find the circumference of a circle given the diameter or radius, and vice versa.
The table shows some examples.

Distance	Formula	Approximate Value (for $\pi \doteq 3.14$)	
Radius	$r = \frac{d}{2}$	5 m	1.5 cm
Diameter	$d = \frac{C}{\pi}$	10 m	3.0 cm
Circumference	$C = \pi d$, $C = 2\pi r$	31.4 m	9.42 cm

Practice

1. Estimate the circumference of each circle with the given diameter.

> **Tip**
> Use $\pi = 3$ for estimates.

a) 2 cm

b) 24 cm

c) 4.2 m

2. Estimate the circumference of each circle with the given radius.

a) 2 cm

b) 24 cm

c) 4.2 m

_____   _____   _____

3. Calculate the circumference of each circle in question 2.
Give the answers to the nearest millimetre.

a) $r = 2$ cm

b) $r = 24$ cm

c) $r = 4.2$ m

_____   _____   _____

4. Calculate the diameter and radius of each circle.
Give the answers to the nearest millimetre.

a) $d =$ _____

b) $d =$ _____

c) $d =$ _____

$r =$ _____

$r =$ _____

$r =$ _____

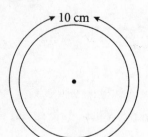
10 cm

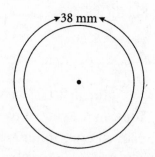
29 cm

38 mm

5. A glass has a circular base with a circumference of 21.4 cm.

a) Calculate the diameter of the circular base. _____

b) Circular coasters are made to extend beyond the edge of the glass base by 1 cm.

What is the diameter of the coaster? _____

c) Calculate the circumference of the coaster. _____

6. A car tire has a radius of 36 cm. A stone gets stuck in the tire. How many times will it hit
the ground when the car travels a distance of 1 km? Show your work.

HINT
Circumference is the
distance around the
car tire.

The stone will hit the ground _____ times.

Quick Review

➤ When a circle is divided into many congruent sectors,
the sectors can be arranged to approximate a parallelogram.

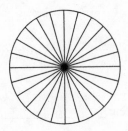 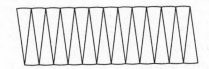

The more congruent sectors we use to divide the circle, the closer the area of the parallelogram is to the area of the circle.

For even larger numbers of sectors, the parallelogram approaches a rectangle.
So, area of circle = area of rectangle

The sum of the 2 longer sides of the rectangle is equal to the circumference, C.
Length of rectangle: $l = \frac{C}{2} = \frac{2\pi r}{2} = \pi r$
Each of the shorter sides is equal to the radius, r.
Width of rectangle: $w = r$

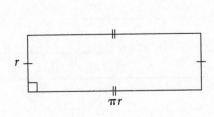 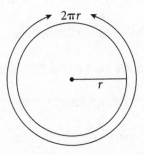

So, the area of a circle with radius, r, is: $A = l \times w = \pi r \times r = \pi r^2$
You can use the formula $A = \pi r^2$ to find the area of any circle given the radius r.

➤ For a circle with radius 1.2 cm, or 12 mm, its area is:
$A = \pi(1.2 \text{ cm})^2 = 1.44\pi \text{ cm}^2$, or $A = \pi(12 \text{ mm})^2 = 144\pi \text{ mm}^2$

This illustrates that when an area in square centimetres has 2 decimal places, the area is given to the nearest square millimetre.

Practice

1. Estimate the area of each circle.

a)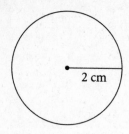
2 cm

b)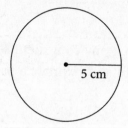
5 cm

c)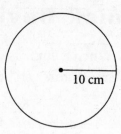
10 cm

Area: _____   Area: _____   Area: _____

2. Calculate the area of each circle in question 1.
Give the answers to the nearest square millimetre.

a) $r =$ _____   b) $r =$ _____   c) $r =$ _____

$A = \pi \times ($ _____ $)^2$

$\doteq$ _____

Area: _____   Area: _____   Area: _____

3. Calculate the area of each circle.
Give the answers to the nearest square millimetre.

a)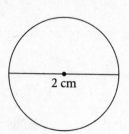
2 cm

b)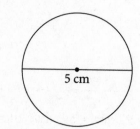
5 cm

c)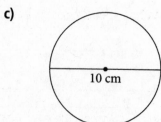
10 cm

$r =$ _____ $r =$ _____ $r =$ _____

Area: _____   Area: _____   Area: _____

4. Use the results of questions 2 and 3.
What happens to the area of a circle when
its radius is doubled?

$\frac{12.57}{3.14} =$ _____ $\frac{314.16}{78.54} =$ _____

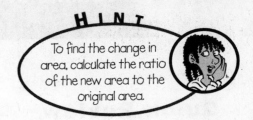

HINT

To find the change in area, calculate the ratio of the new area to the original area.

_____

What happens to the area of a circle when its radius is halved?

$\frac{3.14}{12.57} =$ _____

_____

5. A machine is cutting circular coasters out of specialized foam.

a) Each coaster has a diameter of 12 cm. What is its radius? _____

b) What is the area of each coaster? _____

c) Each piece of foam is a rectangle measuring 144 cm by 984 cm.

What is the area of the foam? _____

d) The coasters are cut with minimum waste.
How many coasters can be cut from each piece of foam?

_____

e) What area of foam is wasted?

_____

6. The circumference of a circle is 92 cm. Calculate the area of the circle.
Give the answer to the nearest square millimetre. Show your work.

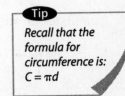

Tip

Recall that the formula for circumference is:
$C = \pi d$

The area of the circle is _____.

Quick Review

➤ A cylinder is a prism with two congruent bases that are circles.

Recall that the formula for the volume of a prism is:
$V = $ base area $\times$ length

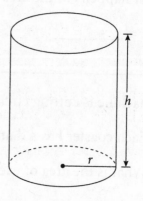

For a cylinder, the base is a circle that has its area given by this formula:
$A = \pi r^2$, where r is the radius of the circle

The height of a cylinder is its length.
So, the volume of a cylinder with height h is:
$V = \pi r^2 \times h$,   or $V = \pi r^2 h$

➤ You can use this formula for the volume of a cylinder to find the capacity of cylindrical containers:

A food can has base radius 4.2 cm and height 3.8 cm. The volume of the can is:
$V = \pi r^2 h$
$\quad = \pi (4.2)^2 \times 3.8$
$\quad \doteq 211$

Since 1 cm³ = 1 mL, the capacity of the food can is about 211 mL.

Practice

Give each volume to the nearest cubic unit.

1. Calculate the volume of this cylinder.

Radius of base: $r = $ _____

Height of cylinder: $h = $ _____

$V = \pi r^2 h$

$\quad = \pi (\underline{\quad\quad})^2 \times \underline{\quad\quad\quad}$

$\quad \doteq \underline{\quad\quad\quad\quad\quad}$

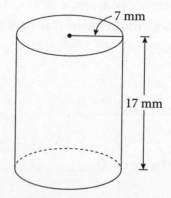

7 mm

17 mm

The volume of the cylinder is _____.

2. Calculate the volume of each cylinder.

a)

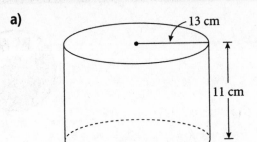

Volume: _____

b)

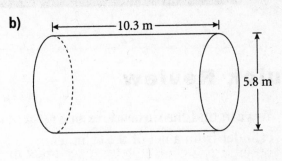

Volume: _____

3. The base of a cylindrical juice container is a circle with diameter 20 cm. The height of the container is 80 cm.

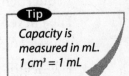

Tip
Capacity is measured in mL.
1 cm³ = 1 mL

a) What is the capacity of the juice container?

The capacity of the juice container is _____.

b) The juice container will be filled to 90% of its capacity. What will be the volume of juice in the container?

_____

c) The juice company decides to use a box to contain the juice. What is the minimum height of the box if its base measures 10 cm by 12 cm?

H I N T
A box is a rectangular prism. Its volume equals base area times height.

_____

4. The main trunk of a tree is in the shape of a cylinder. The distance around its cross section is 47.1 cm and its height is 0.7 m.

a) What is the radius of the cross section? _____

b) What volume of wood is there in the trunk? Show your work.

The volume of wood in the trunk is _____.

Quick Review

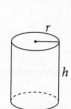

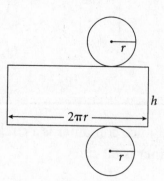

➤ You can find the surface area of a cylinder from a net of the cylinder.

The bases of the cylinder are 2 congruent circles.
The curved surface of the cylinder is a rectangle with width equal to the circumference of the circle, which is $2\pi r$.

So, the surface area, SA, of the cylinder is:
SA = area of 2 congruent circles + area of rectangle

In symbols:
$SA = 2 \times (\pi r^2) + (2\pi r \times h)$
$SA = 2\pi r^2 + 2\pi rh$
where r is the radius of the circular base and h is the height of the cylinder.

➤ You can use this formula: $SA = 2\pi r^2 + 2\pi rh$ to find the area of material needed for producing a cylinder.
In some cases, the surface area of a cylinder is the area of curved surface only.
For example, to find the material needed for a soup-can label, you find the area of the rectangle in the net of the cylinder only.
Curved $SA = 2\pi rh$

Practice

Give each surface area to the nearest square unit.

1. Calculate the surface area of this cylindrical tube.

$SA = 2\pi rh$

     $= 2\pi \times$ _____ $\times$ _____

     $\doteq$ _____

The area of the tube is _____.

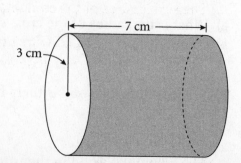

132

2. Calculate the surface area of each cylinder. Show your work.

a)

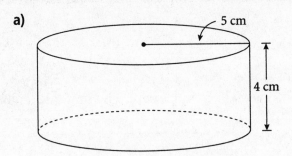

The surface area of the cylinder is _____.

b)

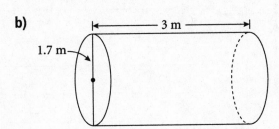

The surface area of the cylinder is _____.

3. A fruit can has diameter 5.8 cm and height 10.5 cm. A plastic label wraps around the can. What is the area of the plastic label?

The area of the plastic label is _____.

4. A cylindrical container has radius 3 cm and height 82 cm.

a) Find the surface area of the container.

The surface area of the container is _____.

b) The container is coated with 2 layers of specialty paint that costs $6.05 per jar. Each jar of paint covers 800 cm². How much does the paint cost?

The paint costs _____.

In Your Words

Here are some of the important words of this unit.
Build your own glossary by recording definitions and examples here. The first one is done for you.

radius _distance between a point on a circle and the centre of the circle_

For example, the radius of this circle is 1 cm.

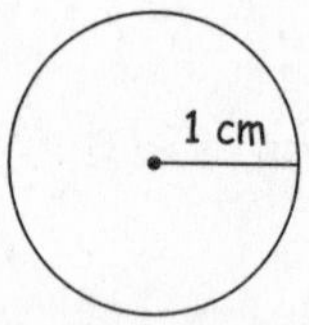

1 cm

diameter

circumference

area of a circle

volume

surface area

List other mathematical words you need to know.

Unit Review

LESSON

6.1 **1.** This circle has the centre at point O.

a) Draw a radius of the circle.

What is the radius of the circle? _____

b) Draw a diameter of the circle.

What is the diameter of the circle? _____

c) Write a relationship between the radius, *r*, and the diameter, *d*, of a circle.

_____

6.2 **2.** Billy plans to put some plastic edging around his circular fish pond. The diameter of the pond is 5 m. Round the answer to the nearest whole-number unit.

a) Find the amount of plastic edging that Billy will need.

_____

b) If plastic edging costs $2.30/m, how much will Billy pay for the edging?

_____

3. During competition, a figure skater must skate a figure **8** twice. The figure **8** is made up of 2 identical circles, each with radius 1.2 m.

a) What is the distance around each of these circles? _____

b) Find the total distance the figure skater has to skate for the competition.

_____

4. The circumference of a circular table is 4.2 m. Find the radius of the table in centimetres.

_____

6.3 **5.** Estimate the area of each circle, then calculate the area to the nearest square unit.

a) radius of 4 mm

Estimate: _____

Area: _____

b) diameter of 10.1 m

Estimate: _____

Area: _____

> **Tip**
> Use $\pi = 3$ in your estimates.

135

6.3 **6.** Find the area of this ring to the nearest square unit. Show your work.

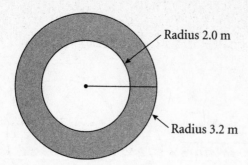

Radius 2.0 m

Radius 3.2 m

The area of the ring is _____.

6.4
6.5 **7.** Find the volume and surface area of this cylinder.

H I N T

Substitute the values of *r* and *h* in the formulas for volume and surface area.

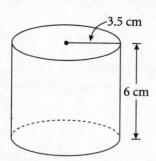

3.5 cm

6 cm

The volume of the cylinder is _____.

The surface area of the cylinder is _____.

8. Use the cylinder in question 7.
A circular hole of diameter 2 cm is drilled
from the centre of the top to the bottom.

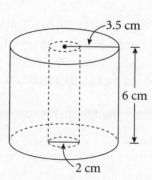

3.5 cm

6 cm

2 cm

a) Find the volume of the new solid.
Give the answer to the nearest cubic unit.

The volume of the new solid is _____.

b) Find the area of the inner surface of the new solid to the nearest square unit.

The area of the inner surface of the new solid is _____.

Geometry

Just for Fun

Split into Four

Use line segments joining vertices to divide this figure into 4 congruent shapes.

How many different shapes can you have?

_____

Show at least 2 ways of doing this.

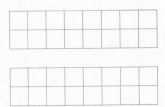

Build from Four

This square is divided into 2 congruent rectangles, each with a diagonal drawn.

Copy the square.
Then cut along
the dashed lines
to get 4 congruent
triangles.

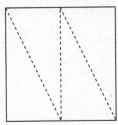

Which of these shapes can you make using all 4 of the triangles?
rectangle, parallelogram, rhombus, trapezoid, kite, triangle

_____

_____

4-Letters or More

A Game for 2 or more

Make as many words as you can from the letters of the word TRANSFORMATION.
Each word has at least 4 letters. A 4-letter word scores 1 point, and
a word with more than 4 letters scores 2 points. No plurals allowed.
The person who scores the most points in 4 min wins.

_____

_____

Skills You'll Need

Using a Protractor to Measure Angles

To measure an angle, place the base line of a protractor along one arm of the angle, with the centre of the protractor on the vertex of the angle.
Read the angle measure from the scale that has its 0 on the arm of the angle.

Example 1

Find the measure of this angle.

Solution

The measure of the angle is 35°.

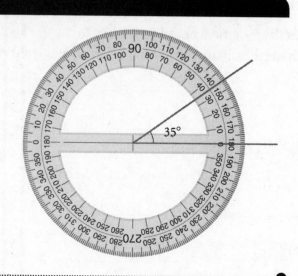

 Check

1. Measure each angle in polygon ABCDE.

   ∠A = 90°   ∠B = _____ °   ∠C = _____ °

   ∠D = _____ °   ∠E = _____ °

   Find the sum of the angles.

   ∠A + ∠B + ∠C + ∠D + ∠E = _____ °

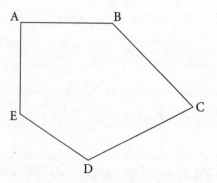

Describing Transformations

There are 3 types of transformations:
A translation moves a figure to a new position by a sliding the figure along a straight line.
A rotation turns a figure about a fixed point, called the turn centre.
A reflection flips a figure over a line, called the mirror line.

Example 2

Describe the transformations of Figure A for which Figures B, C, D, E, and F are images.

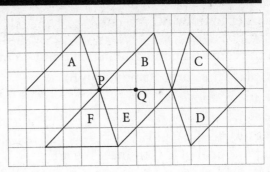

Solution

Figure B is the image of Figure A after a translation of 4 units right.

Figure C is the image of Figure A after a reflection in a vertical line through point Q.

Figure D is the image of Figure A after a rotation of 180° about point Q.

Figure E is the image of Figure A after a rotation of 180° about point P.

Figure F is the image of Figure A after a translation of 1 unit right and 3 units down.

 **Check**

2. Describe the transformation for which:

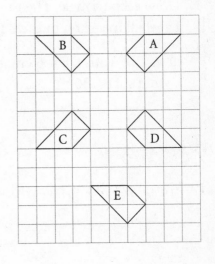

   a) Figure B is the image of Figure A.

   Reflection in a _____ line

   b) Figure C is the image of Figure A.

   _____

   c) Figure D is the image of Figure A.

   _____

   d) Figure E is the image of Figure B.

   _____

Using a Ruler and Compass for Constructions

To construct △ABC with BC = 5 cm, AB = 4 cm, and ∠C = 45°, make a sketch of the triangle first.

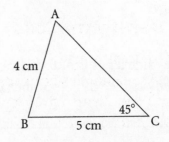

Then follow these steps:

Use a ruler to draw BC = 5 cm.

With the compass point and pencil point 4 cm
apart, place the compass point on B.
Draw an arc above BC.

Use a protractor to draw ∠C = 45°.
Extend one arm of ∠C to meet the arc.
Label the point of intersection A.

Join AB.

Measure AC, ∠A, and ∠B.
AC = 5.3 cm, ∠A = 63°, ∠B = 72°

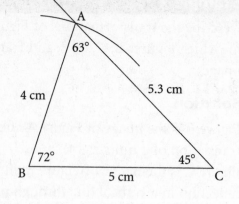

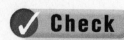

3. Draw each triangle. Then measure the unknown sides and angles.
   Label all measures in each diagram.

Tip

Sketch the
triangle first.

   a) △DEF with DE = 6 cm, EF = 3 cm,   b) △PQR with PQ = 7 cm, QR = 4 cm,
      and ∠D = 30°   and PR = 4 cm

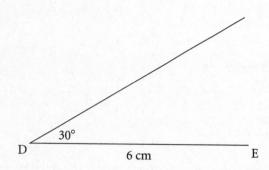

4. A triangle has side lengths of 6 cm, x cm, and 9 cm.
   What are the possible whole-number values of x?

_____

_____

Quick Review

➤ Two angles are **complementary** when they have an angle sum of 90°.

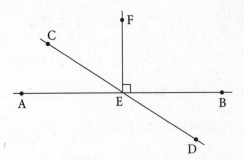

In the diagram, ∠FEB = 90°
∠AEC + ∠CEF = 90°
So, ∠AEC and ∠CEF are complementary.
∠AEC is the complement of ∠CEF and
∠CEF is the complement of ∠AEC.

➤ Two angles are **supplementary** when they
have an angle sum of 180°.

In the diagram, ∠AED + ∠DEB = 180°
So, ∠AED and ∠DEB are supplementary.
∠AED is the supplement of ∠DEB and ∠DEB is the supplement of ∠AED.

Similarly, ∠AEC and ∠CEB are supplementary.
∠AEF and ∠FEB are also supplementary.
In fact, they are equal.

➤ When two lines intersect, the **opposite angles**
are equal.

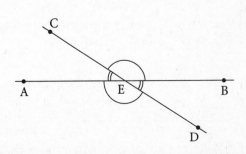

In the diagram, line segments AB and CD
intersect at E.
So, ∠AEC = ∠DEB and ∠AED = ∠CEB.

Practice

1. In this diagram, name an angle that is

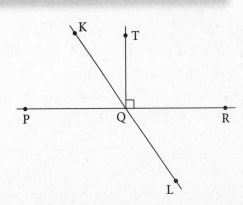

a) supplementary to ∠LQR _____

b) supplementary to ∠PQT _____

c) complementary to ∠KQT _____

d) opposite ∠PQK _____

e) opposite ∠KQR _____

141

2. Find the measures of these angles in the diagram.

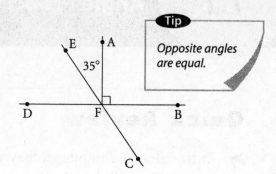

Tip

Opposite angles are equal.

a) $\angle DFE = $ _____

b) $\angle BFC = $ _____

c) $\angle DFC = $ _____

d) $\angle EFB = $ _____

3. Name an angle in this diagram that is

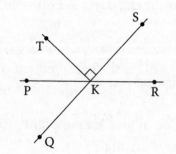

a) equal to $\angle PKQ$ _____

b) complementary to $\angle PKQ$ _____

c) supplementary to $\angle PKQ$ _____

If $\angle PKQ = 25°$, name an angle that is

d) $65°$ _____   e) $155°$ _____

4. a) Sketch a pair of supplementary angles that are equal in measure. Explain.

_____

_____

b) Sketch a pair of complementary angles that are equal in measure. Explain.

_____

_____

c) Sketch a pair of opposite angles that are supplementary. Explain.

_____

_____

d) Sketch a pair of opposite angles that are complementary. Explain.

_____

_____

Quick Review

➤ In any triangle, the sum of the angles in the triangle is 180°.

A triangle can always be considered as one-half of a parallelogram.

In this diagram, △ABC is one-half of parallelogram ABCD, which is translated along AB to position BPQC.

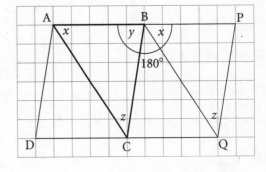

Since the translation is along AB, ABP is a straight line and parallelogram BPQC is identical to parallelogram ABCD.

A straight angle measures 180°.

∠ABC + ∠CBQ + ∠QBP = 180°

Since ∠ABC = y
∠CBQ = ∠DAC = ∠ACB = z
∠QBP = ∠CAB = x
$y + z + x = 180°$

So, in △ABC, ∠A + ∠B + ∠C = 180°

HINT
When there is one angle at the vertex, use a single letter to name the angle.

➤ To find the measures of ∠A, ∠B, or ∠C in △ABC, use the angle sum relationship: ∠A + ∠B + ∠C = 180°

Find the measures of ∠B and ∠C in this diagram.
In △BDE,
∠B + ∠BDE + ∠BED = 180°
∠B + 90° + 30° = 180°
∠B = 180° − 90° − 30°
∠B = 60°

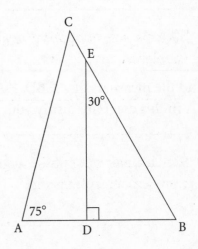

In △ABC,
∠A + ∠B + ∠C = 180°
75° + 60° + ∠C = 180°
∠C = 180° − 75° − 60°
∠C = 45°

Practice

1. Find the measures of ∠B and ∠C in each diagram.

a) ∠B = _____

   ∠C = _____

b) ∠B = _____

   ∠C = _____

Tip

Recall the properties of isosceles triangles.

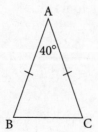

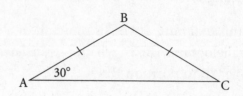

2. Find the measure of each named angle.

a) ∠L = _____

   ∠K = _____

b) ∠VST = _____

   ∠V = _____

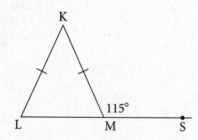

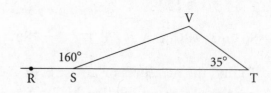

3. Find the measures of ∠CBD, ∠ABD, and ∠A in this diagram. Justify your answers.

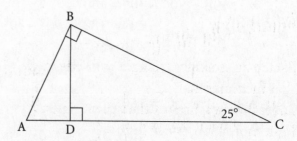

∠CBD = _____   ∠ABD = _____   ∠A = _____

4. Find the measures of ∠R, ∠QTS, and ∠QST
in this diagram. Justify your answers.

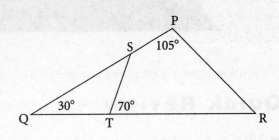

∠R = _____   ∠QTS = _____   ∠QST = _____

5. Find the measures of ∠R and ∠T. Justify your answers.

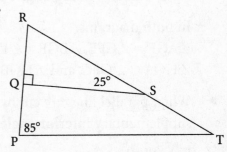

∠R = _____   ∠T = _____

6. ABCDEFGH is a regular octagon.
Find the measure of ∠F. Show your work.

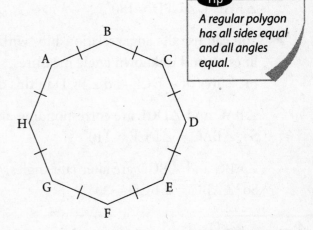

> **Tip**
> A regular polygon
> has all sides equal
> and all angles
> equal.

∠F = _____

7. Sketch an isosceles triangle with one angle
that measures 48°.
Label the measures of the other angles.
Find more than one solution.

Quick Review

➤ When parallel lines are cut by a **transversal**, equal **alternate angles** are formed.

In both diagrams,
$\angle AGF = \angle GFD$ and $\angle BGF = \angle GFC$

➤ When parallel lines are cut by a transversal, equal **corresponding angles** are formed.

In both diagrams,
$\angle AGF = \angle CFE$, $\angle BGF = \angle DFE$,
$\angle HGA = \angle GFC$, and $\angle HGB = \angle GFD$

➤ When parallel lines are cut by a transversal, supplementary **interior angles** are formed.

In both diagrams,
$\angle AGF + \angle GFC = 180°$
$\angle BGF + \angle GFD = 180°$

➤ You can use the angle relationships with parallel lines to find unknown angle measures, such as the measures of $\angle DCE$ and $\angle BCD$ in this diagram.

$\angle BAC$ and $\angle DCE$ are corresponding angles.
So, $\angle BAC = \angle DCE = 110°$

$\angle ABC$ and $\angle BCD$ are alternate angles.
So, $\angle ABC = \angle BCD = 20°$

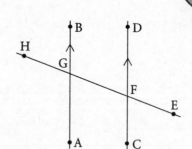

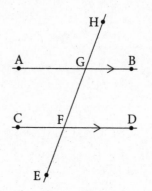

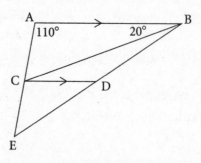

Practice

1. Use the variables to name the angle that is:

a) corresponding to angle a _____

b) alternate to angle q _____

c) an interior angle of angle d _____

d) alternate to angle c _____

e) corresponding to angle r _____

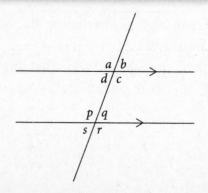

146

2. Find the measure of each angle in this diagram.

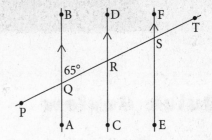

   a) ∠DRS _____   **b)** ∠QRC _____

   c) ∠DRQ _____   **d)** ∠RSE _____

   e) ∠FST _____   **f)** ∠RSF _____

3. Find the measure of each angle in this diagram.

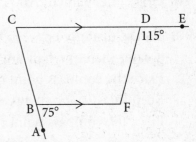

   a) ∠AEF _____   **b)** ∠BEG _____

   c) ∠EGF _____   **d)** ∠CFH _____

H I N T

Review other angle relationships you have learned.

4. a) Find the measures of ∠F and ∠C.

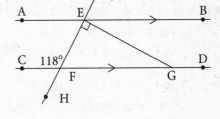

   ∠F _____   ∠C _____

   b) Find the sum of the angles in trapezoid CDFB.
        Show your work.

        The sum of all angles in trapezoid CDFB is _____.

5. In parallelogram PQRS, ∠P = 63°. Find the measures of ∠Q and ∠R. Explain your answers.

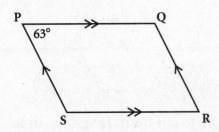

6. Find the measure of ∠P in this diagram. Justify your answer.

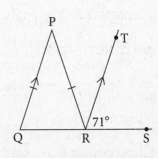

Quick Review

There are different methods that can be used to **bisect** lines and angles.

➤ You can use a ruler and compass to draw the **perpendicular bisector** of a line segment.

i)

ii)
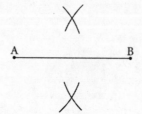

iii)
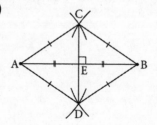

i) Draw line segment AB.

ii) Set the distance between the compass and pencil points to a length greater than one-half the length of AB.
Place the compass point on A. Draw an arc above and below AB.
Keep this distance between the compass and pencil points.
Place the compass point on B. Draw another set of 2 arcs above and below AB to intersect the arcs already drawn.

iii) Label the points C and D where the arcs intersect. Join CD.

CD is the perpendicular bisector of AB.

➤ You can use a ruler and compass to draw the **bisector of an angle**.

i)
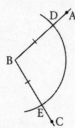

ii)
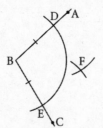

iii)
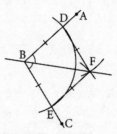

i) Place the compass point on B of ∠ABC. Draw an arc to cut BA in D and BC in E.

ii) Place the compass point on D. Draw an arc between the arms of the angle.
Keep the distance between the compass and pencil points.
Place the compass point on E. Draw an arc to cut the previous arc in F.

iii) Join BF.

BF is the bisector of ∠ABC.

1. Use a ruler and compass to draw each.

a) the perpendicular bisector of AB

b) the bisector of ∠PQR

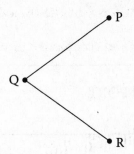

2. △ABC is right angled at B.
Use a ruler and compass to draw the
perpendicular bisectors of AB and BC.
Label point D where the bisectors meet.
Measure DA, DB, and DC.

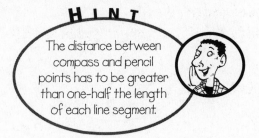

The distance between
compass and pencil
points has to be greater
than one-half the length
of each line segment.

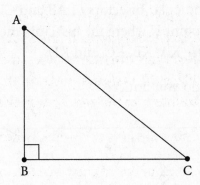

What do you notice?

_____

3. Use a ruler and compass to draw
the bisector KB of ∠ABD.
Then draw the bisector LB of ∠DBC.
Use a protractor to measure ∠KBL.

What do you notice?

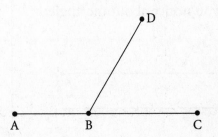

_____

4. In this diagram, PQ = QR.
Use a ruler and compass to construct the
perpendicular bisectors of PQ and QR.
Label point T where the bisectors meet.
Join PT and RT.
Measure TP and TR.

What do you notice?

_____

Describe quadrilateral PQRT.

_____

_____

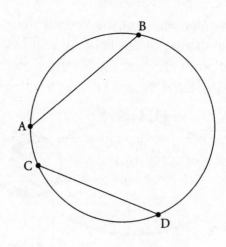

5. AB and CD are line segments with end
points on this circle.
Use a ruler and compass to draw the
perpendicular bisectors of AB and CD.
Label point K where the bisectors meet.
Measure KA, KB, KC, and KD.

What do you notice?

_____

6. Use a ruler and compass to
construct the bisectors of the angles
in △KLM.

What do you notice about the angle
bisectors?

_____

_____

Quick Review

➤ You can use a ruler and a compass to construct angles of specific measures without the use of a protractor.

The construction is based on your knowledge of other geometric constructions. For example,

A 60° angle can be drawn by constructing an equilateral triangle.

A 90° angle can be drawn by constructing the perpendicular bisector of a line segment.

A 30° angle can be drawn by bisecting a 60° angle.

A 45° angle can be drawn by bisecting a 90° angle.

➤ You can construct more angles by drawing the supplementary angle of a constructed angle or by combining angles.

A 120° angle can be drawn as the supplementary angle of 60°, or drawn as two 60° angles with a common arm.
In these diagrams, ∠PRS = 180° − 60° = 120°, ∠BCD = 60° + 60° = 120°

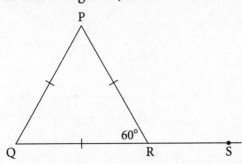
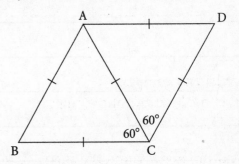

A 135° angle can be drawn as the supplementary angle of 45°, or drawn as a 90° angle and a 45° angle with a common arm.
In these diagrams, ∠NLM = 180° − 45° = 135°, ∠EGH = 45° + 90° = 135°

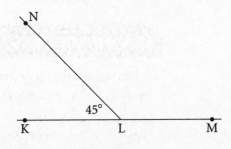
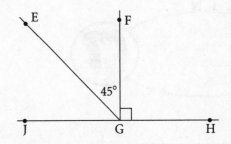

Practice

1. To construct each angle using only a ruler and compass, state how you make use of two other angles for this construction.

   a) 120° _____   **b)** 150° _____

   c) 210° _____   **d)** 105° _____

> **Tip**
> *Write the angle as a sum or a difference of 2 special angles.*

2. An isosceles right △ABC has AB = AC.
   Bisect ∠B and ∠C.
   Label point D where the bisectors meet.

   What is the measure of ∠ACD?

   _____

   What is the measure of ∠BDC?

   _____

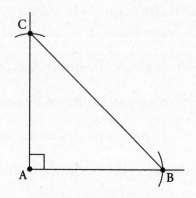

3. Use only a ruler and a compass. Construct a 30°-60°-90° triangle. Explain your steps.

   _____

   _____

   _____

   _____

   _____

   _____

   _____

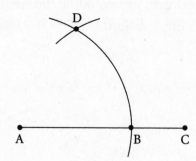

4. Trapezoid ABCD has AB = 6 cm, AD = BC = 4 cm, ∠A = ∠B = 60°.
   Use ruler and compass to construct the trapezoid. Find the measure of ∠DCB and DC.

   HINT
   Make a sketch of the trapezoid first.

   ∠DCB = _____

   DC = _____

152

Quick Review

When solving problems involving angle measurement, you might need to use these angle relationships you have learned in this unit.

➤ For intersecting lines:
Opposite angles are equal.
Two angles that are complementary add to 90°.
Two angles that are supplementary add to 180°.

➤ The sum of angles in a triangle is 180°.
In an isosceles triangle, two sides are equal and two angles are equal.

➤ For a transversal intersecting a set of parallel lines:
Alternate angles are equal.
Corresponding angles are equal.
Interior angles add to 180°.

➤ In this diagram,

Angle sum of triangle: $e + f + 90° = 180°$

Interior angles: a and k

Alternate angles: a and f, d and e

Corresponding angles: a and h, b and k, c and f

Opposite angles: a and c, f and h, g and k

Complementary angles: c and d, a and d, e and f

Supplementary angles: a and b, b and c, f and g, g and h, h and k, f and k

Practice

1. Name two angles in this diagram that are:

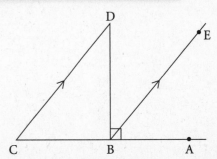

Alternate angles _____

Corresponding angles _____

Complementary _____

Supplementary _____

153

2. Find the measures of ∠BAC and ∠D in this diagram. Justify your answers.

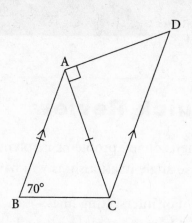

∠ACB = _____ (△ABC is isosceles)

∠BAC = _____ (angle sum of a triangle)

∠ACD = ∠BAC = _____ (alternate angles)

∠D = _____ (_____)

3. In this diagram, explain how you know that △QRS is isosceles with QR = QS.

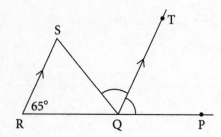

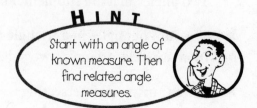

H I N T

Start with an angle of known measure. Then find related angle measures.

∠PQT = ∠SRQ (_____) = _____

4. Find the measures of ∠E, ∠CFE, and ∠CFB. Justify your answers.

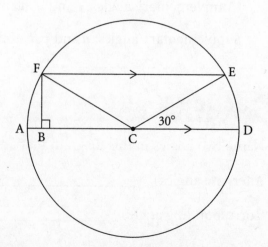

5. Find the measures of ∠CAB, ∠DAC, and ∠D. Justify your answers.

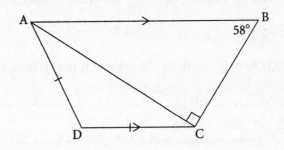

6. Find the measures of ∠LQP, ∠PLQ, ∠KPL, ∠PLK, and ∠PKL in this diagram. Justify your answers.

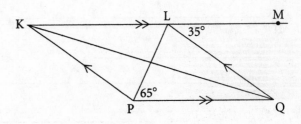

7. Find the values of *x*, *y*, *z*, *w*, and *t* in this diagram. Explain how you know.

Tip

Review angle relationships you have learned in this unit.

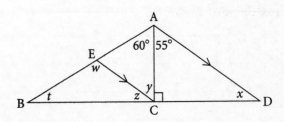

In Your Words

Here are some of the important mathematical words of this unit.
Build your own glossary by recording definitions and examples here. The first one is done for you.

complementary angles *two angles that add up to 90°*
For example, a 32° angle and a 58° angle are complementary.

supplementary angles _____

transversal _____

alternate angles _____

corresponding angles _____

perpendicular bisector _____

List other mathematical words you need to know.

_____

Unit Review

LESSON

7.1   **1.** An angle measures 58°. What is the measure of each of these angles?

  a) Its complementary angle   **b)** Its supplementary angle   **c)** Its opposite angle

  _____   _____   _____

2. Name and find the measure of an angle that is:

  a) complementary to ∠QWR _____

  b) supplementary to ∠RWS _____

  c) opposite to ∠RWS _____

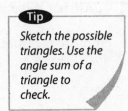

7.2   **3.** An isosceles triangle has one angle that measures 64°.
  What are the measures of the other two angles?
  Find two solutions.

> **Tip**
>
> *Sketch the possible triangles. Use the angle sum of a triangle to check.*

4. Find the measure of each angle in this diagram.
  Justify your answers.

  a) ∠RST = _____

  b) ∠RTS = _____

  c) ∠PQS = _____

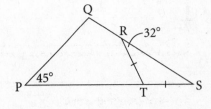

7.3   **5.** Find the measure of each angle. Justify your answers.

  a) ∠DBC = _____

  b) ∠C = _____

  c) ∠CDB _____

  d) ∠DEB _____

  e) ∠BEA _____

  f) ∠EBA _____

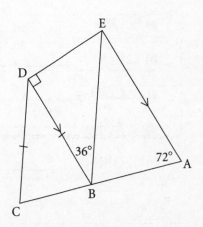

157

7.4 **6.** ∠PQR is an obtuse angle.

Draw the bisector of ∠PQR.
Label it KQ.

Draw the perpendicular bisector of QR.
Label it LM.

Label point A where KQ intersects LM.

What is the measure of ∠QAM?

∠QAM = _____

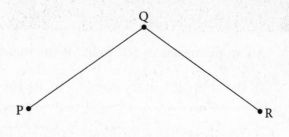

7.5 **7.** Use only a ruler and compass.
Construct trapezoid ABCD with ∠A = ∠B = 30°, AB = 10 cm, and AD = 3 cm.

Find the measure of DC. _____

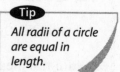

Tip

Make a sketch of trapezoid ABCD first. Start by constructing a 60° angle at point A.

7.6 **8.** Find the measure of each angle. Justify your answers.

a) ∠OBA = _____

b) ∠BOC = _____

c) ∠COD = _____

d) ∠AOB = _____

e) ∠OBC = _____

Tip

All radii of a circle are equal in length.

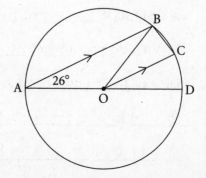

UNIT 8 Square Roots and Pythagoras

Just for Fun

Calculator Challenge

You may use any keys on your calculator.

What is the greatest number you can get using exactly three 2s?

_____

Write the least number you can get using exactly three 2s.

_____

Letter Symmetry

A letter has line symmetry if it can be folded in half with the 2 halves matching each other.

A ⋮ B ⋮

Which letters in the alphabet have more than one line of symmetry?

_____

What Do You Notice?

Try these steps on the number 3087.

1. Use the 4 digits to form the greatest possible number. _____

2. Use the 4 digits to form the least possible number. _____

3. Subtract the least from the greatest. _____

4. Repeat steps 1 to 3 with this result. _____

5. Keep repeating steps 1 to 3 with each result. _____

   What do you notice? _____

Pick any 4-digit number and try again. What do you notice?

_____

_____

Skills You'll Need

Areas of a Square and a Triangle

Area is the amount of surface a figure covers. It is measured in square units.

The formula for the area of a square is: $A = s^2$, where s is the length of a side of the square.

The formula for the area of a triangle is: $A = \frac{1}{2} bh$, where b is the base length and h is the height.

Example 1

Find the area of each figure.

a)

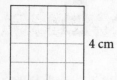

4 cm

b)

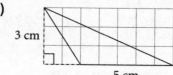

3 cm

5 cm

Solution

a) The figure is a square.
   Substitute $s = 4$ in $A = s^2$.
   $A = (4)^2$
   $\quad = 16$
   The area is 16 cm².

b) The figure is a triangle.
   Substitute $b = 5$ and $h = 3$ in $A = \frac{1}{2} bh$.
   $A = \frac{1}{2} (5 \times 3)$
   $\quad = 7.5$
   The area is 7.5 cm².

✓ Check

1. Find the area of each figure.

a)

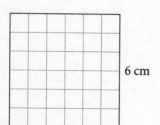

6 cm

b)

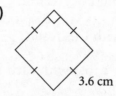

3.6 cm

The area is _____.

The area is _____.

c)

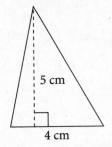

5 cm

4 cm

The area is _____.

d)

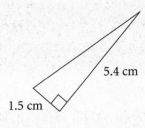

5.4 cm

1.5 cm

The area is _____.

Square Numbers

When a number is squared (multiplied by itself), a **square number** is produced.
This number is also called a **perfect square**.
25 is a square number or a perfect square because $25 = 5 \times 5$, or 5^2.
A square number can be modelled by a square with area equal to the square number.

Example 2

Show that 9 is a square number. Use symbols, words, and a diagram.

Solution

With symbols: $9 = 3 \times 3 = 3^2$
With words: "Nine equals three squared."
So, 9 is a square number.

9 units² | 3 units

3 units

✓ Check

2. Circle the square numbers.

a) 36   b) 12   c) 6   d) 144

3. Complete the statement for each square number.

a) 64 is a square number because $64 = $ _____ $\times$ _____ $= $ _____ ^{2}

b) 121 is a square number because _____ $= $ _____ $\times$ _____ $= $ _____ ^{2}

4. Show that 4 is a square number.
Use symbols, words, and a diagram.

Square Roots

Finding a **square root** is the inverse operation
of squaring.
So, $\sqrt{25} = 5$ because $5^2 = 25$

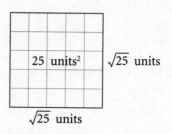

25 units² $\sqrt{25}$ units

$\sqrt{25}$ units

A square root can be modelled using a square.
The area is the square number.
The length of a side of the square is a square root of
the square number.

Example 3

Find a square root of 81.

Solution

Use systematic trial.
Try 8. $8^2 = 64$; 64 is too small.
Try 10. $10^2 = 100$; 100 is too large.
Try 9. $9^2 = 81$; 9 is correct.
So, $\sqrt{81} = 9$

HINT

Think: Does the number,
when multiplied by itself,
produce 81?

✓ Check

5. Complete the statement for each square root.

a) $\sqrt{9} = 3$ because _____$^2 =$ _____

b) $\sqrt{49} = 7$ because _____$^2 =$ _____

c) $\sqrt{100} =$ _____ because _____$^2 =$ _____

d) $\sqrt{144} =$ _____ because _____$^2 =$ _____

6. Find the square number and complete each statement.

a) $\sqrt{} = 4$ because $4^2 =$ _____

b) $\sqrt{} = 8$ because $8^2 =$ _____

c) $\sqrt{} = 13$ because _____ $=$ _____

d) $\sqrt{} = 15$ because _____ $=$ _____

7. Find each square root.

a) $\sqrt{36}$ _____

b) $\sqrt{121}$ _____

c) $\sqrt{196}$ _____

Quick Review

➤ Area of a square = side length × side length
= (side length)^2

When the side length of a square is l, its area is l^2.
When the area of a square is A, its side length is $\sqrt{A}$.

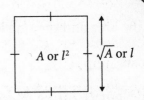

For example,
A square has side length 12 cm.
Its area is: $(12 \text{ cm})^2 = 144 \text{ cm}^2$
A square has area 100 cm^2.
Its side length is: $\sqrt{100}$ cm = 10 cm

➤ The length of any line segment AB on a grid can be found by constructing a square with the segment as one of its sides.
The length of AB is the square root of the area of the square.

To find the area of the square, first find the area of the enclosing square, and then subtract the sum of the areas of the triangles.

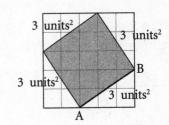

Area of the enclosing square: 5×5 units^2 = 25 units^2
Area of 1 triangle: $\frac{1}{2}(2)(3)$ units^2 = 3 units^2
Area of 4 triangles: 4×3 units^2 = 12 units^2
Area of square with AB as a side: 25 units^2 − 12 units^2 = 13 units^2
So, the length of AB is $\sqrt{13}$ units.
$\sqrt{13}$ is not a whole number because 13 is not a perfect square.

Practice

1. Circle the correct answer for each question.

> **Tip**
> Think: Shall I find the area or the side length?

a) $\sqrt{9}$ 81   3

b) 16^2 256   4

c) $\sqrt{100}$ 10   50

d) $\sqrt{36}$ 18   6

e) 25^2 5   625

2. The area, A, of a square is given. Find the side length of the square.

a) $A = 50$ cm^2

b) $A = 8$ mm^2

c) $A = 169$ cm^2

_____ _____ _____

3. Complete this table.

Side Length of Square	20	21	22			
Area of Square				529	576	625

4. Find the area and the side length for each shaded square.

a) Area: _____

Side length: _____

b) Area: _____

Side length: _____

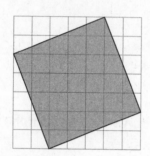

c) Area: _____

Side length: _____

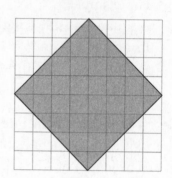

5. Find the length of each line segment.

a) _____

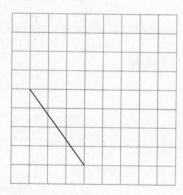

b) _____

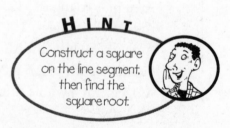

H I N T

Construct a square on the line segment, then find the square root.

c) _____

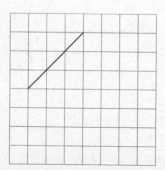

d) _____

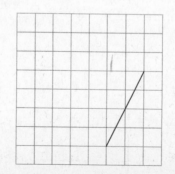

KEY TO SUCCESS

When you have solved some problems, share your work with a classmate for feedback and suggestions. Look for more efficient methods and record them.

Quick Review

➤ You can use a number line to approximate the value of the square root of a number that is not a perfect square.

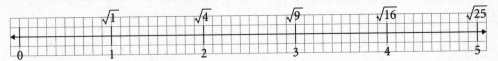

To estimate the value of $\sqrt{10}$:

- Find the square number closest to 10, but greater than 10, which is 16.
- Find the square number closest to 10, but less than 10, which is 9.

Since $\sqrt{9} = 3$ and $\sqrt{16} = 4$, $\sqrt{10}$ must have a value between 3 and 4, but closer to 3.

➤ Use a calculator and systematic trial to get a closer approximation.

Try 3.3: $3.3 \times 3.3 = 10.89$ (too large)
Try 3.2: $3.2 \times 3.2 = 10.24$ (too large)
Try 3.1: $3.1 \times 3.1 = 9.61$ (too small)
Try 3.16: $3.16 \times 3.16 = 9.9856$ (very close)
The approximate value of $\sqrt{10}$ is 3.16.

➤ $\sqrt{10}$ cannot be described exactly by a decimal. The decimal for $\sqrt{10}$ never repeats and never terminates. A number like this is called an **irrational number**.

Practice

1. Use this number line to complete each statement with whole numbers. The first one is done for you.

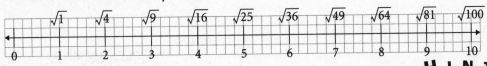

a) $\sqrt{5}$ is between 2 and 3.

b) $\sqrt{20}$ is between _____ and _____.

c) $\sqrt{42}$ is between _____ and _____.

d) $\sqrt{55}$ is between _____ and _____.

e) $\sqrt{2}$ is between _____ and _____.

f) $\sqrt{75}$ is between _____ and _____.

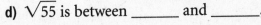

HINT

Find perfect squares close to the number inside the square root symbol.

165

2. Place the letter of each square root on this number line.
The first one is done for you.

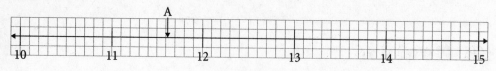

A $\sqrt{135}$ B $\sqrt{201}$ C $\sqrt{108}$ D $\sqrt{167}$ E $\sqrt{188}$

3. Which statements are true and which are false? Explain.

a) $\sqrt{20}$ is between 19 and 21. _____

b) $\sqrt{20}$ is between 4 and 5. _____

c) $\sqrt{20}$ is closer to 4 than 5. _____

d) $\sqrt{20}$ is between $\sqrt{19}$ and $\sqrt{21}$. _____

4. Use a calculator and systematic trial to approximate each square root to 2 decimal places.
Show your work.

a) $\sqrt{20} \doteq$ _____   b) $\sqrt{55} \doteq$ _____   c) $\sqrt{115} \doteq$ _____

5. Find the approximate side length of the square with each area.
Give your answer to the nearest millimetre.

a) $A = 50 \text{ cm}^2$

b) $A = 125 \text{ cm}^2$

> **Tip**
> To round a length
> in centimetres to
> the nearest
> millimetre, you
> round to 1
> decimal place.

6. What length of fencing is required to surround a square field with area 250 m²?
Show your work. Give your answer to the nearest centimetre.

Quick Review

➤ A right triangle has two **legs** that form the right angle. The third side opposite the right angle is called the **hypotenuse**.

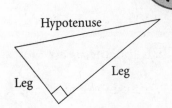

➤ The three sides of a right triangle form a relationship, known as the **Pythagorean Theorem**.

Pythagorean Theorem: The area of the square on the hypotenuse is equal to the sum of the areas of the squares on the legs.

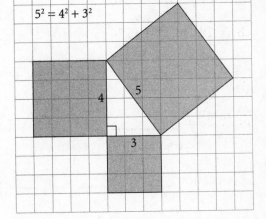

In this diagram,
Area of square on hypotenuse: $5^2 = 25$
Area of squares on legs: $4^2 + 3^2 = 16 + 9$

Notice that: $25 = 16 + 9$, or $5^2 = 4^2 + 3^2$

This relationship is true for all right triangles.

➤ You can use the Pythagorean relationship to find the length of any side of a right triangle when the lengths of the other two sides are known. For example:

To calculate the hypotenuse h, solve for h in this equation.
$h^2 = 7^2 + 10^2$
$h^2 = 49 + 100$
$h^2 = 149$
$h = \sqrt{149}$
Use a calculator. $h \doteq 12.2$

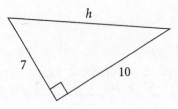

To calculate the side length l, solve for l in this equation.
$$12^2 = l^2 + 9^2$$
$$144 = l^2 + 81$$
$$144 - 81 = l^2 + 81 - 81$$
$$63 = l^2$$
$$l = \sqrt{63}$$
Use a calculator. $l \doteq 7.9$

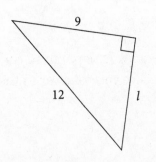

Practice

1. The area of the square on each side of a triangle is given. Is the triangle a right triangle?

a) _____

b) _____

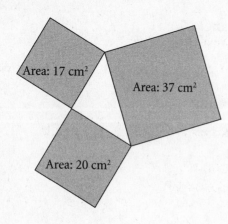

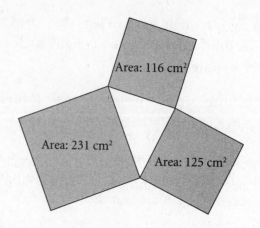

2. The 3 sides of each triangle are given. Tell which triangle is a right triangle. Explain.

a) 3 cm, 4 cm, 5 cm

The triangle is a right triangle

because _____ ^{2} + _____ ^{2} = _____ ^{2}

_____

b) 6 cm, 8 cm, 14 cm

_____

_____

c) 9 cm, 12 cm, 15 cm

_____

_____

_____

d) 5 cm, 12 cm, 13 cm

_____

_____

3. Circle the length of the unknown side in each right triangle.

a) $\sqrt{13}$ $\sqrt{89}$

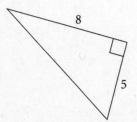

b) $\sqrt{7}$ 5

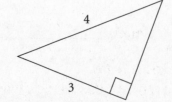

c) $\sqrt{289}$ $\sqrt{161}$

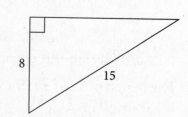

4. Find the length of the hypotenuse in each right triangle.
   Use a calculator to approximate each length to one decimal place.

Tip
Hypotenuse is the side opposite the right angle.

a)

12 cm

10 cm

b)

6 cm

7 cm

Hypotenuse: _____   Hypotenuse: _____

5. Find the length of the unmarked leg in each right triangle.
   Use a calculator to approximate each length to one decimal place.

a)

5 cm

2 cm

b)

6 cm

4 cm

Length of leg: _____   Length of leg: _____

6. Find the length of the unmarked side in each triangle.
   Use a calculator to approximate each answer to one decimal place.

a)

5 cm   5 cm

b)

5 cm

25 cm

H I N T

Think: Is the unmarked side a leg or a hypotenuse?

Length: _____   Length: _____

7. The hypotenuse of a right triangle is $\sqrt{61}$.
   What whole-number lengths of legs can this triangle have? Explain.

_____

_____

Quick Review

At Home At School

➤ The Pythagorean Theorem is true for all right triangles.

You can use this theorem to solve problems involving right triangles.

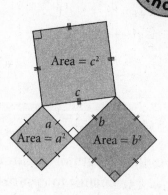

Area = c^2

An algebraic equation for the Pythagorean Theorem is:
$c^2 = a^2 + b^2$
where c is the length of the hypotenuse and a and b are the lengths of the two legs.

Area = a^2 Area = b^2

➤ You can calculate how high up the wall the ladder in the diagram can reach using the formula $c^2 = a^2 + b^2$.
Since the length of the ladder is the hypotenuse of the right triangle, label it c.
The lengths of the two legs of this triangle are labelled a and b.

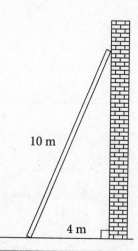

10 m

4 m

The ladder is 10 m long.
The foot of the ladder is 4 m from the wall.
Substitute $b = 4$ and $c = 10$
into the formula $c^2 = a^2 + b^2$.

> **Tip**
> You may label the length of the unknown leg as a or b.

$$10^2 = a^2 + 4^2$$
$$100 = a^2 + 16$$
$$100 - 16 = a^2 + 16 - 16$$
$$84 = a^2$$
$$a = \sqrt{84}$$
$$a \doteq 9.2$$

The ladder can reach about 9.2 m up the wall.

Practice

1. Use the Pythagorean Theorem to check if this is a right triangle.

> **Tip**
> The hypotenuse is the longest side of a right triangle.

Substitute $a =$ _____, $b =$ _____, and $c =$ _____
into the formula $c^2 = a^2 + b^2$.

$c^2 =$ _____ $a^2 + b^2 =$ _____

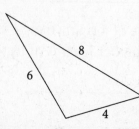

8

6

4

Since c^2 _____ $a^2 + b^2$,

the triangle _____ a right triangle.

2. Use the equation $c^2 = a^2 + b^2$ to find the length of each hypotenuse.
Give the lengths to the nearest millimetre.

a)

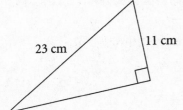

6 cm

10 cm

b)

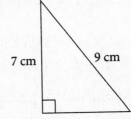

9 cm

5 cm

c)

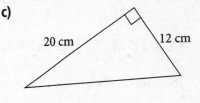

20 cm

12 cm

Hypotenuse: _____

Hypotenuse: _____

Hypotenuse: _____

3. Use the equation $c^2 = a^2 + b^2$ to find the length of each unknown leg.
Give the lengths to the nearest millimetre.

a)

23 cm

11 cm

b)

7 cm

9 cm

c)

30 cm

19 cm

Length: _____

Length: _____

Length: _____

For questions 4 to 8, give each length to 1 decimal place.

4. An 8-m ladder leans against a wall.
The foot of the ladder is 3 m from the base of the wall.
How far up the wall can this ladder reach?
Show your work.

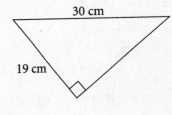

H I N T

Identify which is the
hypotenuse before
your substitution.

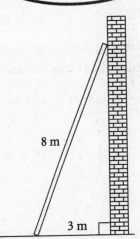

8 m

3 m

The ladder can reach a height of _____.

5. A 6-m ladder is used to reach a window 5 m above ground.
What is the farthest distance from the base of the wall
that the foot of the ladder can rest?

6 m

5 m

The farthest distance is _____.

6. A ramp has height 2 m.
The sloping length of the ramp needs to be 8 m long.
What is the horizontal length of the ramp?

2 m

8 m

The horizontal length of the ramp is _____.

7. A ship leaves port and travels 12 km due north.
It then changes course and travels due east for 10 km.
How far must the ship travel to go directly back to port?
Sketch a diagram to explain.

The ship must travel _____.

8. A rectangular field is 40 m long and 30 m wide.
Carl walks from one corner of the field to the opposite corner along the edge of the field.
Jade walks across the field diagonally to arrive at the same corner.
How much shorter is Jade's shortcut? Show your work.

Tip

Sketch a diagram first.

Jade's shortcut is _____ shorter.

Quick Review

➤ The Pythagorean Theorem can be used to find the area of an isosceles triangle or an equilateral triangle.

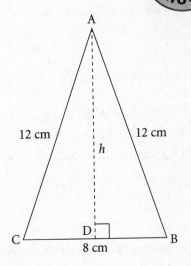

For any triangle, $A = \frac{1}{2} \times base \times height$
The base of isosceles $\triangle ABC$ is 8 cm. Use the Pythagorean Theorem to find the height, h.

Consider right $\triangle ABD$.
Substitute $a = 4$, $b = h$, and $c = 12$
into the formula $c^2 = a^2 + b^2$.

$$12^2 = 4^2 + h^2$$
$$144 = 16 + h^2$$
$$144 - 16 = 16 + h^2 - 16$$
$$128 = h^2$$
$$h = \sqrt{128}$$

The height of $\triangle ABC$ is $\sqrt{128}$ cm.
So, the area of $\triangle ABC = \frac{1}{2} \times 8 \times \sqrt{128}$
$\doteq 45$
The area of $\triangle ABC$ is about 45 cm².

Tip
Use a calculator to find the square root.

➤ The Pythagorean Theorem can also be used to find the volume and surface area of a hexagonal prism.

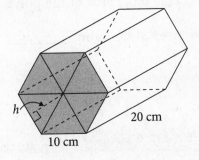

The base of this hexagonal prism has 6 congruent equilateral triangles. The height, h, of one of these triangles can also be calculated using the formula $c^2 = a^2 + b^2$.
$10^2 = 5^2 + h^2$; $75 = h^2$; $h = \sqrt{75}$

The area of one triangle $= \frac{1}{2} \times 10 \times \sqrt{75}$
The area of one hexagonal base is: $6 \times \frac{1}{2} \times 10 \times \sqrt{75} = 30 \times \sqrt{75}$

The length of the prism is 20 cm. So, $V = 30 \times \sqrt{75} \times 20 \doteq 5196$
The volume of the prism is about 5196 cm³.

Tip
To get more accurate results, keep the square root in intermediate steps.

$SA = 2 \times$ area of a hexagonal base $+ 6 \times$ area of a rectangular face
$SA = 2 \times (30 \times \sqrt{75}) + 6 \times (10 \times 20) \doteq 1720$
The surface area of the prism is about 1720 cm².

Give the answers to 1 decimal place if necessary.

1. Use the Pythagorean Theorem to find the height, *h*, of each triangle.

> **Tip**
> *Identify the right triangle that has h as a side length before you apply the Pythagorean Theorem.*

a) Height: _____

b) Height: _____

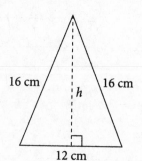

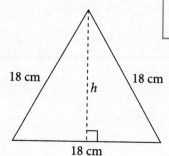

2. Calculate the area of each triangle in question 1.

a) Area: _____

b) Area: _____

3. Each prism has two congruent bases that are regular polygons. Calculate the area of the polygonal base of each prism.

a) Area of hexagon: _____

b) Area of octagon: _____

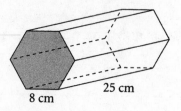

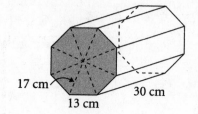

> **Tip**
> *Find how many congruent triangles are in each regular polygon.*

4. Find the volume and surface area of each prism in question 3. Show your work.

a) Volume: _____

Surface Area: _____

b) Volume: _____

Surface Area: _____

In Your Words

Here are some of the important mathematical words of this unit.
Build your own glossary by recording definitions and examples here. The first one is done for you.

perfect square *(square number)*

the product of a whole number multiplied

by itself

For example, 5 multiplied by itself gives

the product 25. 25 is a perfect square.

square root

legs of a right triangle

hypotenuse

Pythagorean Theorem

regular hexagon

List other mathematical words you need to know.

Unit Review

LESSON

8.1 **1.** Simplify without the use of a calculator.

Tip
Use the properties of a square about area and side length.

a) 8^2 _____ b) $\sqrt{49}$ _____ c) 11^2 _____ d) $\sqrt{196}$ _____

2. a) A square has side length 12 cm. Find its area. _____

b) A square has side length 25 cm. Find its area. _____

c) A square has area 225 cm². Find its side length. _____

d) A square has area 30 cm². Find its side length. _____

e) A square has area 120 cm². Find its side length. _____

8.1
8.2 **3.** The side length of each grid square in this diagram is 1 cm.

a) Find the area of the shaded square. _____

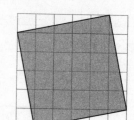

b) What is the side length of the shaded square?

Give your answer as a square root. _____

c) Give the answer in part b to the nearest millimetre. _____

8.2 **4.** Use this number line.

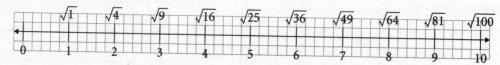

Between which two consecutive whole numbers does each square root lie?

a) $\sqrt{6}$ _____ b) $\sqrt{56}$ _____

c) $\sqrt{78}$ _____ d) $\sqrt{29}$ _____

8.3 **5.** The 3 sides of each triangle are given. Tell which triangle is a right triangle. Explain.

a) 8 cm, 16 cm, 24 cm

b) 15 cm, 20 cm, 25 cm

6. Find the length of the unmarked side in each triangle.
Use a calculator to approximate each answer to 1 decimal place.

a) Length: _____

b) Length: _____

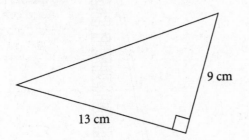

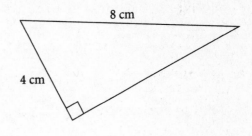

9 cm

13 cm

8 cm

4 cm

7. The hypotenuse of a right triangle is $\sqrt{40}$ units.

a) What whole-number lengths of legs can this
triangle have?

_____

b) Draw a line segment that has the length of
$\sqrt{40}$ units on this grid.

c) What is the area of the square drawn on this
line segment?

_____

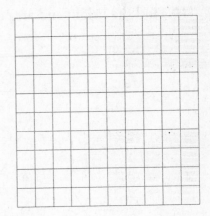

8. Two ships left a port at the same time.
After one hour, one ship was 13 km west of the port,
while the other ship was 15 km south of the port.
How far apart were the two ships after one hour?
Show your work. Give the answer to 1 decimal place.

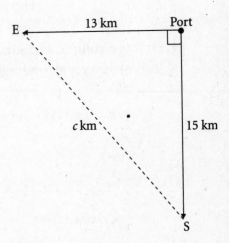

13 km   Port

E

c km   15 km

S

After one hour, the ships were _____ apart.

9. An 11-m ladder leans against a wall.
The foot of the ladder is 2 m from the base of the wall.
How far up the wall can this ladder reach?
Show your work. Give the answer to 1 decimal place.

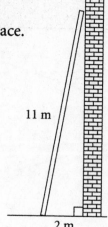

11 m

2 m

The ladder can reach a height of _____.

8.5 **10.** Find the height and area of each triangle. Give the answers to 1 decimal place.

a) Height: _____   **b)** Height: _____

Area: _____   Area: _____

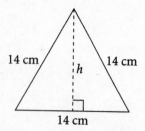

14 cm   14 cm

h

14 cm

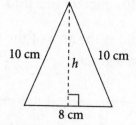

10 cm   10 cm

h

8 cm

11. Find the volume and surface area of this hexagonal prism.
Its base is a regular hexagon. Show your work.

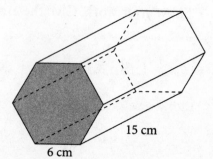

15 cm

6 cm

The volume of the prism is _____.

The surface area of the prism is _____.

Integers

Just for Fun

Modified Sudoku

This is a modified version of a Sudoku puzzle, which originated in Japan.

Complete this grid so that every row, column, and 2 × 3 box contains every digit from 1 to 6.

	1	6			
5					
1		5	4		
6		3	2		5
					4
			1	3	

Cube Count

How many cubes are in this figure? Look for a pattern to find the answer.

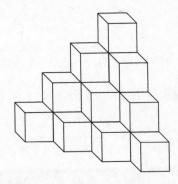

There are _____ cubes.

Add 'Em Up

Find the value of this expression without using a calculator. Explain your work.

$$1 - 2 + 3 - 4 + 5 - 6 + \ldots + 99 - 100 = \underline{\hspace{2cm}}$$

_____

_____

Skills You'll Need

Comparing and Ordering Integers

Positive integers are greater than 0. **Negative integers** are less than 0.
So, positive integers are always greater than negative integers.

You can use a number line to compare and order integers.
On a number line, values increase to the right and decrease to the left.

Opposite integers are the same distance from 0, but are on opposite sides of 0.
For example, –4 and +4 are opposite integers.

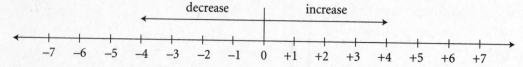

Since –1 is to the right of –4, –1 > –4.   The symbol ">" means "is greater than."
Since –7 is to the left of +3, –7 < +3.   The symbol "<" means "is less than."

You can use these symbols to order integers.

Example 1

Order these integers from least to greatest: +5, –3, +2, 0, –4, –6, +4

Solution

Graph the integers on a number line. Mark a point on the line for each integer.

From least to greatest, read the integers from left to right: –6, –4, –3, 0, +2, +4, +5

✓ Check

1. Complete each statement using one of these words: always, sometimes, never.

   a) A positive integer is _____ greater than a negative integer.

   b) On a number line, an integer is _____ less than any integer to its left.

   c) A negative integer is _____ less than 0.

   d) An integer is _____ greater than its opposite.

2. Use the number line. Order these integers from greatest to least: +6, –3, +2, –5, –1, 0.

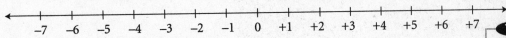

From greatest to least: _____

On a number line, values decrease from right to left.

3. Use > or < to compare each pair of numbers.

a) –5 _____ –9   b) –6 _____ +4   c) 0 _____ –15   d) –7 _____ +6

Using Models to Add Integers

You can use colour tiles to model integers.
A black tile models –1.   A white tile models +1.

■ –1   □ +1

A black tile and a white tile combine to model 0.
They form a **zero pair**: (+1) + (–1) = 0

This is a zero pair.   □ +1
                        ■ –1

Example 2

Use tiles to add.

a) (–4) + (–2)   b) (+5) + (–2)

Solution

Model each integer with tiles and combine the tiles.

a) (–4) + (–2)
   Model –4 with 4 black tiles.
   Model –2 with 2 black tiles.

   There are 6 black tiles altogether.
   They model –6.
   So, (–4) + (–2) = –6

b) (+5) + (–2)
   Model +5 with 5 white tiles.
   Model –2 with 2 black tiles.

   Circle zero pairs.
   3 white tiles remain.
   They model +3.
   So, (+5) + (–2) = +3

181

4. Use tiles to add.

a) $(+1) + (+3) =$ _____

b) $(-2) + (-3) =$ _____

c) $(-4) + (+3) =$ _____

d) $(+4) + (-2) =$ _____

5. Add. Use tiles if they help.

a) $(+2) + (-2) =$ _____

b) $(+11) + (-5) =$ _____

c) $(+7) + (+9) =$ _____

d) $(-3) + (-8) =$ _____

e) $(-12) + (+5) =$ _____

f) $(+7) + (-15) =$ _____

Using Models to Subtract Integers

To add, you combine tiles.
To subtract, you take away tiles.

Example 3

Use tiles to subtract. $(-4) - (-3)$

Solution

Model the first integer.
Take away tiles that represent the second integer.

Model −4 with 4 black tiles.
To subtract −3, take away 3 black tiles.

1 black tile remains. It models −1.
So, $(-4) - (-3) = -1$

If there are not enough tiles to remove, add zero pairs.

Use tiles to subtract. $(-3) - (+2)$

Solution

Model -3 with 3 black tiles.
To take away $+2$, 2 white tiles are needed.
Add 2 zero pairs of tiles to provide 2 white tiles.

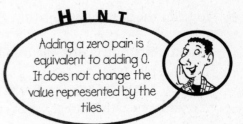

> **HINT**
> Adding a zero pair is equivalent to adding 0. It does not change the value represented by the tiles.

5 black tiles remain. They model -5.
So, $(-3) - (+2) = -5$

✓ **Check**

6. Use tiles to subtract.

   a) $(+3) - (+2) =$ _____

   b) $(+5) - (-3) =$ _____

   c) $(-2) - (+2) =$ _____

   d) $(-1) - (-3) =$ _____

7. Subtract. Use tiles if they help.

   a) $(-9) - (+2) =$ _____

   b) $(-8) - (-7) =$ _____

   c) $(-3) - (+7) =$ _____

   d) $(+2) - (+3) =$ _____

   e) $(+3) - (-1) =$ _____

   f) $0 - (+3) =$ _____

Quick Review

➤ You can use a number line to add integers.

Find the first integer on the number line.

• To add a positive integer, move right on the number line.
• To add a negative integer, move left on the number line.

To add: (−4) + (+2)
Start at −4.
Move 2 units right for adding +2.

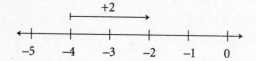

The arrow ends at −2.
So, (−4) + (+2) = −2

To add: (+5) + (−4)
Start at +5.
Move 4 units left for adding −4.

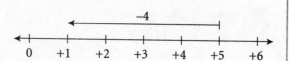

The arrow ends at +1.
So, (+5) + (−4) = +1

➤ When you use a calculator to add integers, look for the (−) or +/− key.

• You use the (−) key to input the negative sign of the negative number.
• You use the +/− key to change an input number to a negative number.

Practice

1. A number line is used to add integers.
Write the addition expression and sum modelled by each diagram.

a) (+3) + (+4) = _____

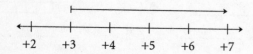

b) (−3) + (_____) = _____

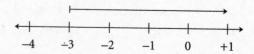

c) _____

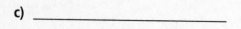

d) _____

2. Add. Use a number line if it helps.

a) $(+12) + (-3) =$ _____

b) $(-4) + (+4) =$ _____

c) $(-6) + (+5) =$ _____   **d)** $(-6) + (+7) =$ _____   **e)** $(-4) + (+13) =$ _____

f) $(+9) + (+8) =$ _____   **g)** $(-8) + (-3) =$ _____   **h)** $(+7) + (-15) =$ _____

3. Complete each addition equation and concluding statement.

a) $(+2) + (+7) =$ _____

$(+3) + (+4) =$ _____

$(+8) + (+5) =$ _____

$(+10) + (+6) =$ _____

When you add 2 positive integers,

the sign of the sum is _____.

b) $(-2) + (-7) =$ _____

$(-3) + (-4) =$ _____

$(-8) + (-5) =$ _____

$(-10) + (-6) =$ _____

When you add 2 negative integers,

the sign of the sum is _____.

4. Complete each addition equation and concluding statement.

a) $(-2) + (+7) =$ _____

$(-3) + (+4) =$ _____

$(+8) + (-5) =$ _____

$(+10) + (-6) =$ _____

b) $(+2) + (-7) =$ _____

$(+3) + (-4) =$ _____

$(-8) + (+5) =$ _____

$(-10) + (+6) =$ _____

c) $(+2) + (-2) =$ _____

$(-3) + (+3) =$ _____

$(-8) + (+8) =$ _____

$(+6) + (-6) =$ _____

When you add a positive integer and a negative integer, the sum is:

• positive when the numerically larger integer is _____.

• negative when the numerically larger integer is _____.

• zero when the integers are _____.

> **Tip**
>
> *The numerical value of an integer is its value without the sign. The numerical value of +3 is 3 and the numerical value of −2 is 2.*

185

5. Without adding, state if each sum is positive, negative, or zero.

a) (–8) + (–2)

b) (–5) + (+1)

c) (+3) + (–3)

_____

_____

_____

d) (–2) + (+7)

e) (+3) + (–12)

f) (+6) + (–3)

_____

_____

_____

6. Use a calculator to add.

a) (+45) + (–145)

b) (–832) + (+238)

c) (–492) + (+953) + (–641)

_____

_____

_____

7. Write an expression that describes the changes in each situation. Then find the sum.

a) The initial temperature is +2°C. Later, the temperature increases by 3°C and then drops 8°C.

HINT

Show the changes on a number line.

(+2) + (_____) + (_____)

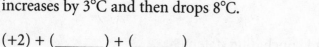

The final temperature is _____ °C.

b) An elevator is initially at level P2 that is 2 floors below ground level. The elevator goes up 7 floors, up 6 more floors, then down 4 floors, and up 1 floor.

(–2) + (_____) + (_____)+ (_____) + (_____)

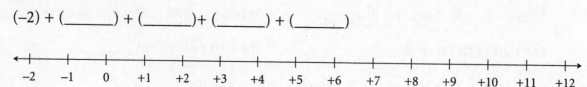

The elevator ends up on the _____ floor.

8. Complete each grid so that every row, column, and diagonal has the same sum. All integers in each grid are different.

a) Sum: _____

0		+2
	–1	
		–2

b) Sum: _____

	–2	–1
–4		+4
	+2	

186

Quick Review

➤ Addition and subtraction are opposite operations.

➤ To subtract an integer on a number line, move in the opposite direction of adding the same integer.

Adding Integers	Subtracting Integers
To add a positive integer, move right.	To subtract a positive integer, move left.
To add a negative integer, move left.	To subtract a negative integer, move right.

To add: $(-4) - (+2)$
Start at -4.
Move 2 units left for subtracting $+2$.

To subtract: $(+5) - (-4)$
Start at $+5$.
Move 4 units right for subtracting -4.

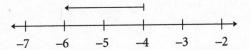

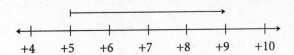

The arrow ends at -6.
So, $(-4) - (+2) = -6$

The arrow ends at $+9$.
So, $(+5) - (-4) = +9$

➤ Subtracting an integer is the same as adding the opposite integer.
The opposite of $+2$ is -2.

$(-4) - (+2) = (-4) + (-2)$
$\qquad\qquad\quad = -6$

$(+5) - (-4) = (+5) + (+4)$
$\qquad\qquad\quad = +9$

Practice

1. Each number line in this chart models a subtraction of integers. Complete the chart.

Number Line	Subtraction Equation	Addition Equation
0 +1 +2 +3 +4 +5	$(+1) - (-3) = $ _____	$(+1) + $ _____ $ = $ _____
−7 −6 −5 −4 −3 −2		$(-3) + (-2) = $ _____
−7 −6 −5 −4 −3 −2		

2. Rewrite each as an addition expression and evaluate.

a) $(+7) - (+3) = (+7) + (-3)$

= _____

b) $(-6) - (+9) = (-6) + (-9)$

= _____

c) $(+8) - (+12) = (+8) +$ _____

= _____

d) $(-7) - (+2) = (-7) +$ _____

= _____

e) $(-2) - (+9) =$ _____

= _____

f) $(-10) - (+10) =$ _____

= _____

> **Tip**
> Subtracting an integer is the same as adding the opposite integer.

When you subtract a positive integer, the result is less than the original integer because

subtracting a positive integer is the same as adding _____.

3. Rewrite as an addition expression and evaluate.

a) $(+2) - (-7) = (+2) + (+7)$

= _____

b) $(-3) - (-4) = (-3) + (+4)$

= _____

c) $(-5) - (-5) =$ _____

= _____

d) $(+10) - (-4) =$ _____

= _____

When you subtract a negative integer, the result is greater than the original integer

because _____

4. Match each description with the correct subtraction expression and answer.

Temperature Change	Expression	Answer
From 8°C to 3°C	$(-3) - (-8)$	−11
From 8°C to −3°C	$(-3) - (+8)$	−5
From −8°C to 3°C	$(+3) - (+8)$	+5
From −8°C to −3°C	$(+3) - (-8)$	+11

> **Tip**
> To find the change, subtract the first integer from the second.

5. Use a calculator to subtract.

a) $(+98) - (+21) - (-456)$

_____

b) $(-73) - (+28) + (-149)$

_____

c) $(-492) - (-953) - (+641)$

_____

Quick Review

➤ You can write a positive integer without the use of the + sign.
+3 can simply be written as 3.
So, all whole numbers are integers.

➤ You can interpret the addition or subtraction of integers without writing the integers in brackets.
Adding –3 is the same as subtracting +3, or subtracting 3.
So, + (–3) can be written as – (+3), or simply – 3.
Adding (+5) + (–3) is the same as finding the difference of 5 – 3.

Subtracting +3 is the same as subtracting 3.
So, – (+3) can be written as – (3), or simply – 3.
Subtracting (–2) – (+3) is the same as finding the difference of –2 – 3.

➤ You can use a number line or mental math to evaluate sums and differences of integers.

Number Line:

$-2 + 3$

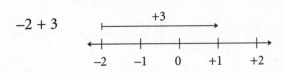

$-2 - 3$

Mental Math:
One number is positive and the other is negative. The answer is the difference between 2 and 3, which is 1. Since 3 is numerically larger, the difference has the same sign as 3.
So, $-2 + 3 = 1$

Both numbers are negative. The answer is the sum of 2 and 3, which is 5. The sign should match the sign of both numbers.
So, $-2 - 3 = -5$

Practice

1. Rewrite each expression without brackets. Then evaluate.

   a) $(+3) + (+6)$

   $= 3 + 6$

   = _____

   b) $(+5) + (+10)$

   = _____

   = _____

   c) $(-5) + (-10)$

   = _____

   = _____

2. Use your results in question 1 to complete these statements.

To add 2 positive integers or 2 negative integers mentally,

find the _____ of their numerical values.

The sign of the answer matches the sign of _____ numbers.

3. Rewrite each expression without brackets. Then evaluate.

a) (−3) + (+6)

$= -3 + 6$

= _____

b) (−5) + (+10)

= _____

= _____

c) (−12) + (+23)

= _____

= _____

d) (+3) + (−6)

= _____

= _____

e) (+5) + (−10)

= _____

= _____

f) (+12) + (−23)

= _____

= _____

4. Match each addition expression with its equivalent expression and answer.

(+8) + (−5)	8 + 5	−3
(+8) + (+5)	−8 − 5	3
(−8) + (−5)	−8 + 5	13
(−8) + (+5)	8 − 5	−13

5. Follow the arrows to find the missing numbers.

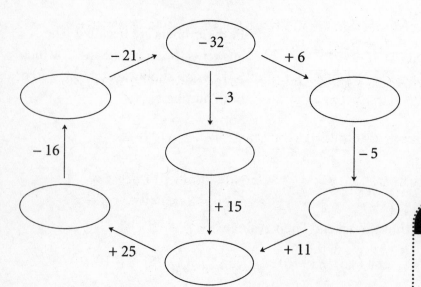

KEY TO SUCCESS

Never be afraid of asking questions in class. Other students may want the same answers to solve their problems or they may share their methods with you.

Quick Review

➤ You can use colour tiles to represent the multiplication of integers.

A black tile models –1. ■   A white tile models +1. □

2 groups of 3 black tiles model 2 × (–3) = –6

–3:
–3:

➤ Integers have these properties of whole numbers.

• **Multiplying by 0:** 4 × 0 = 0 and 0 × 4 = 0
So, (–4) × 0 = 0 and 0 × (–4) = 0

• **Multiplying by 1:** 4 × 1 = 4 and 1 × 4 = 4
So, (–4) × (+1) = –4 and (+1) × (–4) = –4

• **Order Property:** 4 × 2 = 8 and 2 × 4 = 8
So, (–4) × (+2) = –8 and (+2) × (–4) = –8

• **Distributive Property:** 4 × (2 + 3) = 4 × 2 + 4 × 3 = 20
So, (–4) × [(+2) + (+3)] = (–4) × (+2) + (–4) × (+3) = –20

➤ You can write the product of integers without the use of the × sign.
(–4) × (+2) can simply be written as: (–4)(+2)

➤ When 2 integers with the same sign are multiplied, their product is positive.
(+2)(+3) = +6   (–2)(–3) = +6

When 2 integers with different signs are multiplied, their product is negative.
(+2)(–3) = –6   (–2)(+3) = –6

When 2 or more integers are multiplied, count negative signs to find
the sign of the product.

An even number of negative
signs gives a positive product.

An odd number of negative
signs gives a negative product.

(–1)(+2)(–3) = +6

(–1)(–2)(–3) = –6

2 negative signs, so
the product is positive

3 negative signs, so
the product is negative

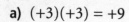

1. Find a pattern rule for each multiplication pattern.
Extend the pattern 3 more rows.

H I N T

To find a pattern rule,
look for a pattern in the
first integer factors and
in the products.

a) $(+3)(+3) = +9$

$(+2)(+3) = +6$

$(+1)(+3) = +3$

$(0)(+3) =$ _____

$(\underline{\hspace{1cm}})(+3) =$ _____

_____

_____

b) $(-3)(+3) = -9$

$(-3)(+2) = -6$

$(-3)(+1) = -3$

$(-3)(0) =$ _____

_____

_____

_____

2. In this chart, write the sign of each product of multiplying 2 integers.

×	positive integer	negative integer
positive integer		
negative integer		

• When 2 integer factors have the same sign, their product is _____.

• When 2 integer factors have different signs, their product is _____.

3. Find each product. The answers form a magic square.

Tip

*In a magic square,
the numbers in
each row, column,
and diagonal have
the same sum. This
sum is called the
magic sum.*

$(-1)(+7)$	$(+1)(+4)$	$(-6)(0)$	$(-1)(-5)$
$(-7)(-1)$	$(+2)(-1)$	$(-1)(-2)$	$(+5)(-1)$
$(+2)(+3)$	$(+1)(-1)$	$(+3)(+1)$	$(+3)(-2)$
$(-2)(+2)$	$(-1)(-1)$	$(-1)(+3)$	$(-2)(-4)$

The magic sum is _____.

4. Find each product.

a) $(-2)(+5)$ _____

b) $(+6)(-5)$ _____

c) $(-3)(-4)$ _____

d) $(+5)(+4)(+3)$ _____

e) $(-1)(-2)(-3)$ _____

f) $(+6)(-1)(+1)$ _____

g) $(0)(-1)(-2)(-3)$ _____

h) $(+1)(-1)(+1)(-1)(+1)$ _____

> **Tip**
>
> To multiply more than 2 integers, start by multiplying the first 2 integers.

5. Write each product in expanded form and complete the pattern.

$(-2)^1 = -2$

$(-2)^2 = (-2) \times (-2) =$ _____

$(-2)^3 =$ _____ $\times$ _____ $\times$ _____ $=$ _____

$(-2)^4 = (-2) \times (-2) \times (-2) \times (-2) =$ _____

$(-2)^5 =$ _____ $\times$ _____ $\times$ _____ $\times$ _____ $\times$ _____ $=$ _____

$(-2)^6 =$ _____ $\times$ _____ $\times$ _____ $\times$ _____ $\times$ _____ $\times$ _____ $=$ _____

- When you multiply an odd number of negative integers, the product is _____.

- When you multiply an even number of negative integers, the product is _____.

6. Without multiplying, name the sign of each product.

a) $(-2)(+5)(-7)$ _____

b) $(+6)(-5)(+2)$ _____

c) $(-3)(-4)(-2)$ _____

d) $(-5)(+4)(-3)(+2)$ _____

e) $(-1)(-2)(-3)(-4)$ _____

f) $(+6)(-1)(+1)(+2)$ _____

7. Match each pattern rule with the corresponding pattern.
Complete each pattern and pattern rule.

Number Pattern	Pattern Rule
$-3, +9, -27, +81, \ldots$	Start at 2. Multiply by _____ each time.
$+2, -10, +50, -250, \ldots$	Start at 1. Multiply by -10 each time.
$+3, -3,$ _____, _____, $\ldots$	Start at _____. Multiply by -3 each time.
$+1, -10,$ _____, _____, $\ldots$	Start at 3. Multiply by -1 each time.
$-1, -2, -4, -8, -16, \ldots$	Start at -1. Multiply by _____ each time.

Quick Review

➤ For any multiplication of 2 different factors, there are 2 related division facts:
For $4 \times 3 = 12$, the related division facts are: $12 \div 3 = 4$ and $12 \div 4 = 3$

The same rules apply to the product of 2 integers.
For $(-2)(+5) = -10$, the related division facts are:

$(-10) \div (-2) = +5$ and $(-10) \div (+5) = -2$

dividend   divisor   quotient

➤ The quotient of 2 integers with the same sign is positive.
$(+10) \div (+2) = +5$ $\qquad$ $(-10) \div (-2) = +5$

➤ The quotient of 2 integers with different signs is negative.
$(+10) \div (-2) = -5$ $\qquad$ $(-10) \div (+2) = -5$

Practice

1. For each product, complete the 2 related division facts and name the sign of the quotient.

Multiplication Fact	Related Division Facts	Sign of Quotient
$(+2)(+3) = +6$	$(+6) \div (+2) = $ _____	_____
	$(+6) \div (+3) = $ _____	_____
$(-2)(-3) = +6$	$(+6) \div (-2) = $ _____	_____
	$(+6) \div (-3) = $ _____	_____
$(+2)(-3) = -6$	$(-6) \div (+2) = $ _____	_____
	$(-6) \div (-3) = $ _____	_____
$(-2)(+3) = -6$	$(-6) \div (-2) = $ _____	_____
	$(-6) \div (+3) = $ _____	_____

2. Use your results in question 1. Complete these 2 statements.

When 2 integers have the same sign, their quotient is _____.

When 2 integers have different signs, their quotient is _____.

3. Find a pattern rule for each division pattern.
Extend the pattern 3 more rows.

HINT

To find a pattern rule, look for a pattern in the dividends and in the quotients.

a) $(+6) \div (-2) = -3$

$(+4) \div (-2) = -2$

$(+2) \div (-2) = -1$

$(0) \div (-2) = \underline{\hspace{2cm}}$

_____

_____

_____

b) $(-12) \div (-4) = +3$

$(-8) \div (-4) = +2$

$(-4) \div (-4) = +1$

$(0) \div (-4) = \underline{\hspace{2cm}}$

_____

_____

_____

Use the last 3 rows of each pattern. Complete these statements.

When both the dividend and divisor are negative, the quotient is _____.

When the dividend is positive and the divisor is negative, the quotient is _____.

4. Complete each pattern or pattern rule.

a) Start at 250. Divide by −5 each time. $+250, -50, \underline{\hspace{1.5cm}}, \underline{\hspace{1.5cm}}$

b) Start at −16. Divide by +2 each time. $-16, \underline{\hspace{1.5cm}}, \underline{\hspace{1.5cm}}, \underline{\hspace{1.5cm}}$

c) Start at _____. Divide by _____ each time. $-192, +48, -12, +3, \ldots$

d) Start at −2. Divide by −1 each time. $\underline{\hspace{1.5cm}}, \underline{\hspace{1.5cm}}, \underline{\hspace{1.5cm}}, \underline{\hspace{1.5cm}}$

e) Start at _____. Divide by _____ each time. $+2000, +200, +20, +2, \ldots$

5. Use 2 of these 5 integers. Write a division fact with each quotient.

$-2 \qquad +3 \qquad +12 \qquad -1 \qquad +4$

a) a quotient of −2   _____

b) the greatest quotient   _____

c) the least quotient   _____

d) a quotient between −5 and −10   _____

6. Use a calculator to divide.

Tip
Look for the [−] or [+/−] key on your calculator to key in negative numbers.

a) $(+247) \div (-13) = \underline{\hspace{2cm}}$ **b)** $(-851) \div (-37) = \underline{\hspace{2cm}}$

c) $(-748) \div (-68) = \underline{\hspace{2cm}}$ **d)** $(-1485) \div (+33) = \underline{\hspace{2cm}}$

Quick Review

➤ The order of operations with whole numbers also applies to integers.

① Perform operations in brackets first.
② Evaluate exponents.
③ Divide and multiply, in order, from left to right.
④ Add and subtract, in order, from left to right.

Tip

The word BEDMAS can help you remember the order of operations.
B–Brackets
E–Exponents
DM–Divide, Multiply
AS–Add, Subtract

$$\overset{① \quad ②④ \quad ③}{(1 + 2)^2 - 3 \times 4}$$

① B $\qquad = (3)^2 - 3 \times 4$
② E $\qquad = 9 - 3 \times 4$
③ DM $\qquad = 9 - 12$
④ AS $\qquad = -3$

➤ A fraction bar indicates division.
It also acts like brackets.
Evaluate the numerator and denominator separately before dividing.

For example, $\frac{12 + 8}{2 - 6} = \frac{20}{-4} = -5$

Practice

1. Simplify.

a) $5 - 2 - 6$

$= \underline{\hspace{1.5cm}} - 6$

$= \underline{\hspace{2cm}}$

b) $3(8 - 12)$

$= 3 \times \underline{\hspace{1.5cm}}$

$= \underline{\hspace{2cm}}$

Tip

Brackets symbolize multiplication as well as grouping.
3(8 – 12) means
3 × (8 – 12).

c) $-4 + 2 \times 3$

$= -4 + \underline{\hspace{1.5cm}}$

$= \underline{\hspace{2cm}}$

d) $21 \div (-7) \times 5$

$= \underline{\hspace{2.5cm}}$

$= \underline{\hspace{2.5cm}}$

e) $10 - [(5 - 3) + 9]$

f) $-8 + 15 \div (-3) + 7$

g) $(-3)(-8) + 24 \div (-2)$

2. Match each expression with its answer.

Expression	Answer
$30 \div (5 - 10) \times 2$	-14
$30 \div (5 - 10 \times 2)$	-12
$(30 \div 5 - 10) \times 2$	-8
$30 \div 5 - 10 \times 2$	-2

3. Simplify.

a) $\dfrac{3(5 - 9)}{2}$

$= \dfrac{3(\underline{\qquad})}{2}$

$= \underline{\qquad\qquad}$

$= \underline{\qquad\qquad}$

b) $\dfrac{(-4)^2}{-8}$

$\underline{\qquad\qquad}$

c) $\dfrac{(-6)(4) + 8}{(-2)^3}$

$\underline{\qquad\qquad}$

4. Evaluate each expression. Write the letter for the answer in the corresponding blank at the bottom to find out what one wall said to the other.

$2(-7 + 3)$ $= 2\underline{\qquad}$ $= \underline{\qquad}$ **A**	$-8 + 12 \div 4$ $= -8 + \underline{\qquad}$ $= \underline{\qquad}$ **C**	$3(10 \div 2) - (-4)$ $= 3\underline{\qquad} + \underline{\qquad}$ $= \underline{\qquad}$ $= \underline{\qquad}$ **E**
$(9 - 3)^2 \div (-4)$ **H**	$4 \times (-3) + 24 \div 2$ **M**	$-5 + 12 \div 4 \times (-2)$ **N**
$19 - 3 \times 4 \div (-6)$ **O**	$\dfrac{6(-8)}{-12} - 1$ **R**	$\dfrac{10 - 2(-3)}{3^2 - 1}$ **T**

$\overline{0}\ \overline{19}\ \overline{19}\ \overline{2}\quad \overline{0}\ \overline{19}\quad \overline{-8}\ \overline{2}\quad \overline{2}\ \overline{-9}\ \overline{19}\quad \overline{-5}\ \overline{21}\ \overline{3}\ \overline{-11}\ \overline{19}\ \overline{3}$

Quick Review

At Home
At School

➤ A **coordinate grid** is formed when a horizontal number line and a vertical number line intersect at right angles at 0.

➤ The horizontal number line is the **x-axis**. The vertical number line is the **y-axis**. They meet at the **origin**.

➤ The axes divide the grid into 4 **quadrants** numbered 1, 2, 3, and 4 counterclockwise.

➤ Points on the axes do not belong to any quadrant.

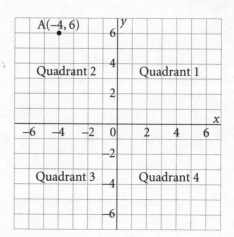

➤ A point on a coordinate grid is located by an **ordered pair** of numbers. The first number, the x-coordinate, tells how far left or right of the origin the point is. The second number, the y-coordinate, tells how far up or down the origin the point is. For example, $(-4, 6)$ is located 4 units left of and 6 units up the origin.

Practice

1. Use each letter once. Complete these descriptions for points in the diagram.

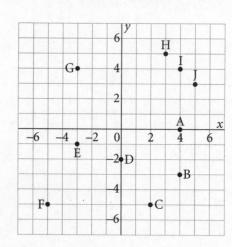

   a) Point _____ is 3 units right of and 5 units up the origin.

   b) Point _____ is 5 units right of and 3 units up the origin.

   c) Point _____ has x-coordinate 0.

   d) Point _____ has y-coordinate 0.

   e) Points _____ and _____ have the same x-coordinates.

   f) Points _____ and _____ have equal x- and y- coordinates.

   g) Points _____ and _____ are in Quadrant 4.

2. Use the diagram in question 1.
Write the coordinates of each point.

HINT
Find how far left/right of the origin and then how far up/down.

a) A (4, _____)

b) B (_____ , –3)

c) C _____

d) D _____

e) E _____

f) F _____

g) G _____

h) H _____

i) I _____

j) J _____

3. Plot these points on the grid.

(2, –9), (0, –5), (–4, –7), (–6, –10),

(–8, –10), (–9, –8), (–7, 0), (–5, 5),

(–6, 7), (–3, 6), (2, 3), (4, 0), (8, –4)

Join the points in the order listed.

What animal did you draw?

_____

4. Graph each set of points. Join the points in order. Then join the last point to the first point.
Name the geometric figure you drew.

a) (5, 3), (5, –3), (–5, –3), (–5, 3)

b) (–4, 0), (2, 0), (5, 3), (–1, 3)

_____   _____

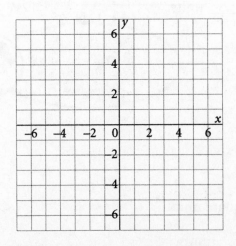

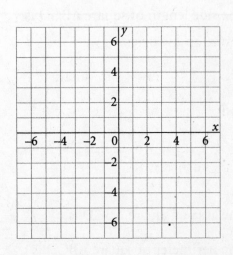

c) (−3, 4), (2, 4), (4, −2), (−4, −2)

d) (5, 1), (−2, −2), (−5, 1), (−2, 4)

_____

_____

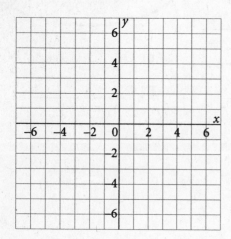

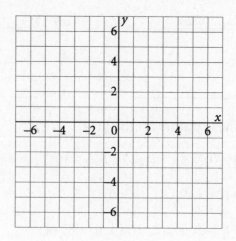

5. a) A(−4, −2), B(−4, 5), and C(3, 5) are 3 vertices of square ABCD.
Graph these points on the grid.

b) What are the coordinates of point D?

_____

Graph this point on the grid.
Join the points to form square ABCD.

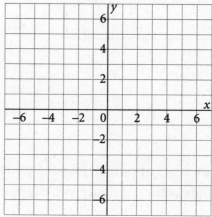

c) Find the area and perimeter of square ABCD.

The side length of square ABCD is _____ units.

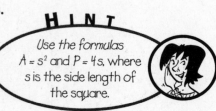

HINT

Use the formulas
$A = s^2$ and $P = 4s$, where
s is the side length of
the square.

The area of square ABCD is _____ square units.

The perimeter of square ABCD is _____ units.

Quick Review

➤ A translation moves a figure in a straight line.
The figure and its image have the same size and shape, and face the same direction.

When the figure is on a square grid, the
translation is described by movements
right or left and up or down.

△A′B′C′ is the image of △ABC after a
translation 7 units left and 4 units up.

Both △ABC and its translation image
△A′B′C′ are read clockwise.

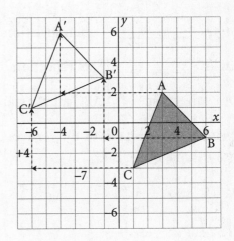

➤ A reflection creates a mirror image of a figure.
The mirror line is a line of symmetry for the figure and its image.

The figure and its image have the same size and shape, but face opposite directions.

△A′B′C′ is the image of △ABC after a reflection in the x-axis.
△A″B″C″ is the image of △ABC after a reflection in the y-axis.

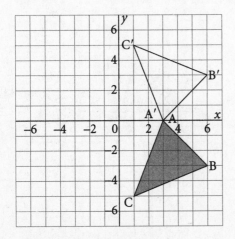

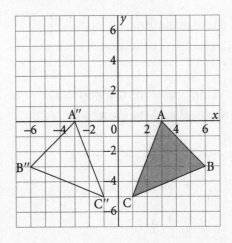

△ABC is read clockwise.
Its reflection images △A′B′C′ and △A″ B″ C″ are read counterclockwise.

201

Practice

1. Which triangles are translation images of the original triangle? Which are reflection images?

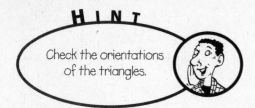

Check the orientations of the triangles.

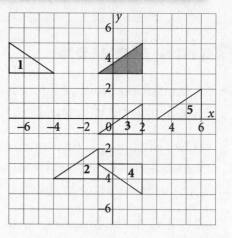

Triangles _____ are translation images.

Triangles _____ are reflection images.

2. a) Draw the image of △ABC after a translation of 5 units left and 3 units up.

b) Write the coordinates of the vertices of △ABC and its image △A'B'C'.

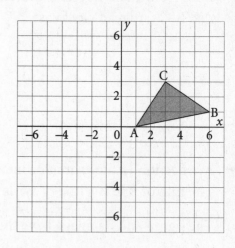

A(1, 0) → A'(–4, 3)

B(6,1) → B'_____

C_____ → C'_____

c) For a translation 5 units left and 3 units up,

the x-coordinate _____ by 5,

and the y-coordinate _____ by 3.

3. Quadrilateral W'X'Y'Z' is a translated image of quadrilateral WXYZ.

a) Describe the translation.

_____

b) Write the coordinates of the vertices of the quadrilateral and its image.

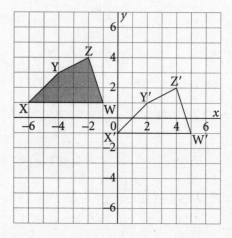

W_____ → W'_____

X_____ → X'_____

Y_____ → Y'_____

Z_____ → Z'_____

4. a) Draw the image of quadrilateral KLMN.
• after a reflection in the *y*-axis. Label the image K′L′M′N′.
• after a reflection in the *x*-axis. Label the image K″L″M″N″.

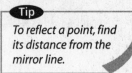
Tip
To reflect a point, find its distance from the mirror line.

b) Write the coordinates of the vertices of KLMN and its image K′L′M′N′.

K_____ → K′_____

L_____ → L′_____

M_____ → M′_____

N_____ → N′_____

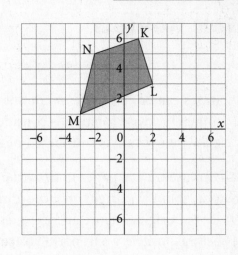

c) Write the coordinates of the vertices of KLMN and its image K″L″M″N″.

K_____ → K″_____   L_____ → L″_____

M_____ → M″_____   N_____ → N″_____

d) Complete each statement about reflection.

When a point is reflected in the *y*-axis, its *y*-coordinate _____

and its *x*-coordinate _____.

When a point is reflected in the *x*-axis, its *x*-coordinate _____

and its *y*-coordinate _____.

5. a) Draw the image of △ABC after a reflection in the line through P(−3, −3), O(0, 0), and R(3, 3).

b) Write the coordinates of the vertices of △ABC and its image △A′B′C′.

A_____ → A′_____

B_____ → B′_____

C_____ → C′_____

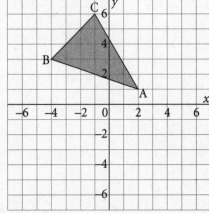

c) What pattern do you see in the coordinates of each point and its image?

_____

_____

Quick Review

➤ A rotation turns a figure about a turn centre.

➤ Rotations can be clockwise or counterclockwise.
A counterclockwise rotation is considered positive.
A clockwise rotation is considered negative.

➤ You can use tracing paper to draw the images of figure after a 90°, 180°, or 270°
rotation about the origin on a coordinate grid.
• Trace the original figure and the axes.
• Label the positive y-axis on the tracing paper.
• Place a pencil point at the origin. Rotate the tracing paper counterclockwise until
the positive y-axis coincides with the given axis.

Rotation	Positive y-axis coincides with . . .
90°	negative x-axis
180°	negative y-axis
270°	positive x-axis

• Mark the vertices of the image with a sharp pencil through the tracing paper.
• Join the vertices to draw the image of the original figure.

This diagram shows the images of a figure after rotations of 90°, 180°, and 270° about
the origin.

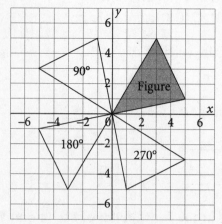

➤ The size and shape of a figure is not changed after a rotation.
The image is congruent to the original figure.

1. Match the image with each transformation of the original figure.

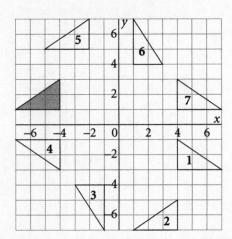

HINT

Reflections change the orientation of a figure, but translations and rotations do not.

Image	Transformation of Original Figure
1	rotation of 90° counterclockwise about the origin
2	reflection in the x-axis
3	translation 2 units right and 4 units up
4	reflection in the y-axis
5	rotation of 180° clockwise about the origin
6	rotation of 90° clockwise about the origin
7	translation 8 units right and 8 units down

2. a) Draw the image of quadrilateral WHAT after a rotation of 90° about the origin.

b) Write the coordinates of the vertices of the original figure and its image.

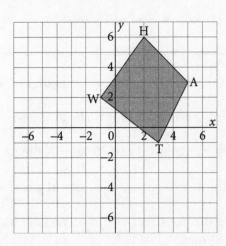

W_____ → W'_____

H _____ → H'_____

A _____ → A'_____

T _____ → T'_____

What pattern do you see in the coordinates?

_____

_____

3. a) Draw the image of quadrilateral WHAT after a rotation of 180° about the origin on the coordinate grid in question 2.

b) Write the coordinates of the vertices of the original figure and its image.

W_____ → W″_____

H _____ → H″_____

A _____ → A″_____

T _____ → T″_____

What pattern do you see in the coordinates?

_____

_____

4. a) Draw the image of quadrilateral WHAT after a rotation of −90° about the origin on the coordinate grid in question 2.

> **Tip**
>
> *A clockwise rotation is shown by a negative angle. −90° is the same as 270°.*

b) Write the coordinates of the vertices of the original figure and its image.

W_____ → W‴_____

H _____ → H‴_____

A _____ → A‴_____

T _____ → T‴_____

What pattern do you see in the coordinates?

_____

_____

5. Use the patterns from questions 2 to 4 to predict the coordinates of the image of K(−5, 1)

a) after a rotation of 90° about the origin. _____

b) after a rotation of 180° about the origin. _____

c) after a rotation of 270° about the origin. _____

6. Write the coordinates of the vertices of the image of △ABC after a rotation of 90° about the origin.

A(3, 2) → A′_____   B(5, −4) → B′_____   C(−6, −1) → C′_____

In Your Words

Here are some of the important mathematical words of this unit.
Build your own glossary by recording definitions and examples here. The first one is done for you.

positive integer *a whole number greater than 0*
For example, 1, 2, 3, ... are positive integers.

negative integer

opposite integers

zero pair

coordinate grid

ordered pair

List other mathematical words you need to know.

Unit Review

LESSON

9.1 **1.** Use <, >, or = to compare each pair of sums.

a) $(-14) + (+8)$ _____ $(-2) + (-3)$ b) $(-1) + (-8)$ _____ $(-11) + (+1)$

2. Each row, column, and diagonal in this grid has the same sum.

		+3	-2
	+1		-3
			-5

a) Complete the grid with integers between -6 and +6. All integers in this grid are different.

b) What is the sum? _____

9.2 **3.** Write the subtraction expression and difference modelled by this diagram.

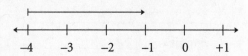

_____

4. Subtract.

a) $(-2) - (+5) =$ _____   b) $(-6) - (+6) =$ _____   c) $(-3) - (-8) =$ _____

5. The temperature in St. John's is -9°C. The temperature in Victoria is +7°C.

What is the difference in temperature between the 2 cities? _____

9.3 **6.** Evaluate.

a) $4 - 7 =$ _____   b) $-12 - 5 =$ _____   c) $-3 + 14 =$ _____

7. The temperature in Calgary at 9 a.m. was -23°C.
By 11 a.m., it had warmed up by 8°C.
By noon, it had warmed up by another 3°C.
But by 2 p.m., it had cooled by 6°C.
What was the temperature in Calgary at 2 p.m.?

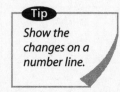

Tip

Show the changes on a number line.

_____

9.4 **8.** Complete each statement using *positive* or *negative*.
The product of a positive integer and a negative integer is _____.

The product of two negative integers is _____.

9. Find each product.

  a) $(+2)(+3) =$ _____

  b) $(-6)(+4) =$ _____

  c) $(-2)(-2)(+3) =$ _____

  d) $(-4)(-5)(-1) =$ _____

  e) $(-1)(+2)(-3)(+4)(-5)(+6) =$ _____

9.5 **10.** Evaluate each quotient and order the results from least to greatest.

  a) $(-20) \div (+4) =$ _____

  b) $(-18) \div (-6) =$ _____

  c) $(+48) \div (-8) =$ _____

The quotients from least to greatest are: _____

11. Write the next 3 terms in each pattern. Then write the pattern rule.

  a) $-128, 64, -32, 16,$ _____, _____, _____, . . .

Pattern rule: Start at _____. _____ each time.

  b) $-3125, -625, -125,$ _____, _____, _____, . . .

Pattern rule: Start at _____. _____ each time.

9.6 **12.** Evaluate.

  a) $17 - 4 \times 4$

  $=$ _____

  b) $-48 \div 4 - 2(3 - 4)$

  $=$ _____

Remember to use the order of operations, BEDMAS.

  c) $(-2)^3 - 4$

  $=$ _____

  d) $\dfrac{(-6)(8-2)}{-4}$

  $=$ _____

  e) $13 + 5 - (-2)(6 - 7)$

  $=$ _____

  f) $\dfrac{21 + 2(3)}{(-3)^2}$

  $=$ _____

9.7   **13.** Use the diagram at the right.

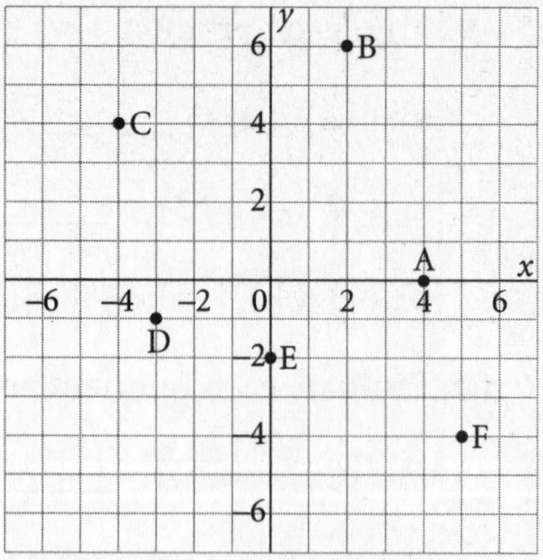

   a) The coordinates of D are _____.

   b) The coordinates of F are _____.

   c) Point _____ has coordinates (2, 6).

   d) The coordinates of the origin are _____.

   e) Point _____ has y-coordinate 0.

   f) Point _____ has x-coordinate 0.

   g) Point _____ is in Quadrant 2.

9.8
9.9   **14.** Plot these points on the coordinate grid:
   A(0, 4), B(6, 5), and C(7, −2).
   Join the points to form △ABC.
   On the same grid, draw the image of
   △ABC after each transformation.

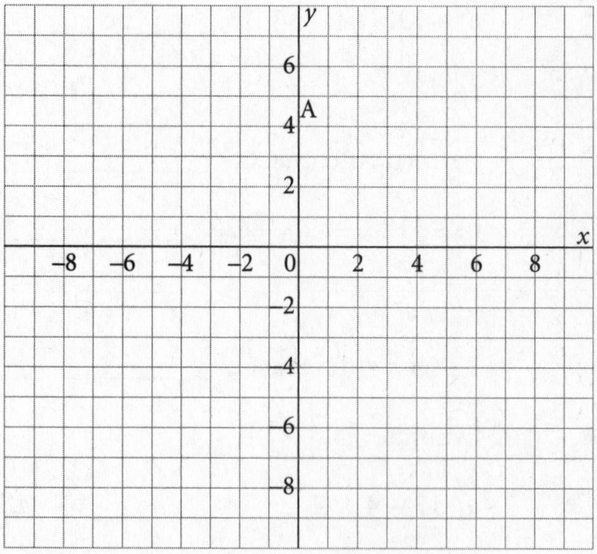

   a) A translation 9 units left and 7 units
      down
      Label the image △A′B′C′.
      Write the coordinates of the vertices
      of △A′B′C′.

      A′_____   B′_____   C′_____

   b) A reflection in the y-axis
      Label the image △A″B″C″. Write the coordinates of the vertices of △A″B″C″.

      A″_____   B″_____   C″_____

   c) A rotation of 90° clockwise about the origin
      Label the image △A‴B‴C‴.
      Write the coordinates of the vertices
      of △A‴B‴C‴.

      A‴_____   B‴_____   C‴_____

   Tip
   A clockwise
   rotation is
   shown by a
   negative angle
   such as
   −90°.

   How are the images alike? Different?_____

   _____

   _____

Just for Fun

Surgeon's Instruction

To find out what the surgeon said, follow these steps:

1. Find the list of words in the word search table on the right.
   Words can be horizontal, vertical, or diagonal.

   ALGEBRA TILE, ALGEBRAIC,

   BALANCE, DISTRIBUTIVE,

   EQUAL, EQUATION,

   EVALUATE, EXPAND,

   ISOLATE, PATTERN, SOLVE,

   SUBSTITUTE, SYMBOL,

   TRIAL, VARIABLE, VERIFY

P	E	R	C	I	A	R	B	E	G	L	A
F	O	R	M	E	T	A	U	L	A	V	E
E	T	U	T	I	T	S	B	U	S	L	T
D	I	S	T	R	I	B	U	T	I	V	E
N	N	R	E	T	T	A	P	T	A	E	Q
A	L	H	E	S	A	R	A	R	M	R	U
P	O	E	E	O	P	R	I	E	R	I	A
X	B	Q	A	T	B	A	I	A	O	F	T
E	M	U	N	E	B	O	N	B	L	Y	I
O	Y	A	G	L	T	H	S	I	D	E	O
S	S	L	E	I	S	O	L	A	T	E	N
B	A	L	A	N	C	E	E	V	L	O	S

2. Write all unused letters in order, row by row, from left to right.

   _____

   _____

3. Insert space between words to write the surgeon's instruction.

   _____

Skills You'll Need

Writing Expressions and Equations

You can use algebraic expressions to represent word statements.

In an algebraic expression, a letter, such as x or n, is used to represent a number. This letter is called a variable.

Multiplication of a number and a letter is written as the number followed by the letter. For example, $4n$ means $4 \times n$.

An equation is a statement that two algebraic expressions are equal. One of them can be a number. For example, $4n = 8$ is an equation and $4n = 10 - n$ is also an equation.

Example 1

a) Write an algebraic expression for this statement:
Five times a number minus 3

b) Write an equation for this sentence:
Three less than five times a number is 2.

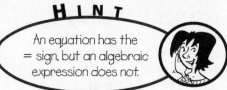

HINT

An equation has the = sign, but an algebraic expression does not.

Solution

Let x be the number.

a) Then, five times a number is $5x$.
$5x$ minus 3 is: $5x - 3$
$5x - 3$ is an algebraic expression.

b) Three less than five times the number is 2.
So, $5x - 3 = 2$
$5x - 3 = 2$ is an equation.

 **Check**

1. Write an algebraic expression for each statement.

   a) eight more than a number _____

   b) two less than seven times a number _____

   c) a number divided by 6 _____

2. Write an equation for each sentence.

   a) The sum of 10 and a number is 15. _____

   b) The product of a number and nine is 63._____

   c) Eleven decreased by 2 times a number is 1. _____

Evaluating Expressions

To find the value of an expression, replace each variable with its given value.
Then use the order of operations to simplify.

Example 2

Evaluate the expression $3a + 2b - 5c$ for $a = \frac{1}{3}$, $b = -2$, and $c = \frac{2}{5}$.

Solution

Substitute $a = \frac{1}{3}$, $b = -2$, and $c = \frac{2}{5}$ into the expression.

$$
\begin{aligned}
3a + 2b - 5c &= 3(\tfrac{1}{3}) + 2(-2) - 5(\tfrac{2}{5}) \\
&= 3 \times \tfrac{1}{3} + 2 \times (-2) - 5 \times \tfrac{2}{5} \qquad \text{Multiply first.} \\
&= 1 + (-4) - 2 \qquad\qquad\qquad\qquad \text{Then add and subtract in order.} \\
&= -5
\end{aligned}
$$

✓ Check

3. Evaluate each expression.

a) $x - 9$ for $x = -5$

$x - 9 = \underline{\quad} - 9$

$= \underline{\qquad\qquad}$

b) $-4x$ for $x = \frac{3}{4}$

$-4x = -4(\underline{\quad})$

$= \underline{\qquad\qquad}$

c) $-6 + x$ for $x = \frac{1}{3}$

$-6 + x = -6 + \underline{\quad}$

$= \underline{\qquad\qquad}$

4. Evaluate each expression for $m = -3$ and $n = \frac{1}{2}$.

a) $m - 2n$

$= \underline{\quad} - 2(\underline{\quad})$

$= \underline{\quad} - \underline{\quad}$

$= \underline{\qquad\qquad}$

b) $3m + 2n$

$= 3(\underline{\quad}) + 2(\underline{\quad})$

$= \underline{\qquad\qquad\qquad}$

$= \underline{\qquad\qquad\qquad}$

c) $4mn$

$= 4(\underline{\quad})(\underline{\quad})$

$= \underline{\qquad\qquad}$

$= \underline{\qquad\qquad}$

5. Evaluate each expression.

a) $a - 4b + 5c$, when $a = 3$, $b = -1$, and $c = -2$. $\underline{\qquad\qquad}$

b) $-2a + 3b + c$, when $a = \frac{1}{4}$, $b = \frac{2}{3}$, and $c = \frac{1}{2}$. $\underline{\qquad\qquad}$

Quick Review

➤ These properties for numbers also apply to variables.
* **Adding 0:** Adding 0 does not change the number.
  $4 + 0 = 4$ and $n + 0 = n$; $0 + 4 = 4$ and $0 + n = n$
* **Multiplying by 0:** When 0 is a factor, the product is always 0.
  $4 \times 0 = 0$ and $n \times 0 = 0$; $0 \times 4 = 0$ and $0 \times n = 0$
* **Multiplying by 1:** When 1 is a factor, the product is always the other factor.
  $4 \times 1 = 4$ and $n \times 1 = n$
  $1 \times 4 = 4$ and $1 \times n = n$
* **Order of Addition and Multiplication:**
  When you add or multiply, the order does not matter.
  $4 + 2 = 6$ and $2 + 4 = 6$ $a + b = b + a$
  $4 \times 2 = 8$ and $2 \times 4 = 8$ $a \times b = b \times a$ and $ab = ba$
* **Distributive Property:**
  $4 \times (2 + 3) = 4 \times 2 + 4 \times 3 = 20$
  $a(b + c) = a \times (b + c) = a \times b + a \times c = ab + ac$
  When you use the distributive property, you **expand**.

➤ The distributive property of multiplication can be illustrated with a diagram.

Area of rectangle = Area of A + Area of B
$$= ab + ac$$

Area of rectangle = length $\times$ width
$$= (b + c)a \text{ or } a(b + c)$$

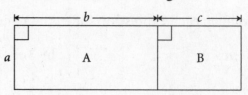

Practice

1. Label each diagram to show the distributive property of multiplication.

a) $6(k + 4) = 6k + 6 \times$ _____   b) $3(8 + y) =$ _____   c) $7(2t + 5) =$ _____

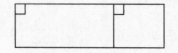
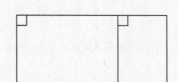

6

2. Use the distributive property of multiplication.
Complete the expansion of each expression.

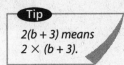
Tip
2(b + 3) means
2 × (b + 3).

    a) $4(b + 9) =$ _____$(b) +$ _____$(9) =$ _____$b +$ _____

    b) $12(7 + d) =$ _____ $+$ _____ $=$ _____

    c) _____$(w + 2) = 8(w) + 8(2) =$ _____

    d) $9($_____$) = 9(5) + 9(3z) =$ _____

3. Expand.

H I N T
When you use the
distributive
property, you
expand.

    a) $6(h + 5)$ **b)** $11(4k + 7)$

       $=$ _____ $=$ _____

       $=$ _____ $=$ _____

    c) $5(13 + 2n)$ **d)** $3(x + 4y + 5)$ **e)** $7(3m + 2n + 1)$

       $=$ _____ $=$ _____ $=$ _____

       $=$ _____ $=$ _____ $=$ _____

4. Write the product and the expanded expression illustrated by each diagram.

    a) _____   **b)** _____

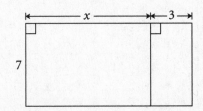
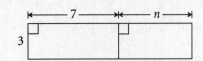

5. Are the two expressions in each pair equivalent expressions? Explain.
For expressions that are not equivalent, change the second expression to make them equivalent.

    a) $6(k + 3)$ and $6k + 9$ _____

    _____

    b) $5(a + 2)$ and $10 + 5a$ _____

    _____

    c) $7(4 + n)$ and $7n + 4$ _____

    _____

Quick Review

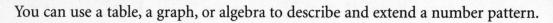

You can use a table, a graph, or algebra to describe and extend a number pattern.

Look at this pattern: 2, 5, 8, 11, ...

To find the 10th term, you can use these 3 methods:

➤ Make a table. Then extend the table to find the 10th term.
The pattern rule is: Start at 2. Add 3 each time.
From the table, the 10th term is 29.

Term Number	1	2	3	4	5	...	10
Term Value	2	5	8	11	14	...	29

➤ Graph the pattern.
Plot the term number on the horizontal axis
and the term value on the vertical axis.
If the points lie on a straight line, use a ruler
to draw a line through the points.
Extend the line to the right to the 10th term.
From the graph, the 10th term is 29.

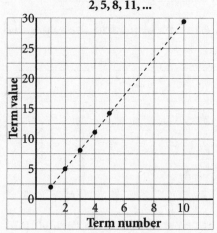

**Graph of Number Pattern
2, 5, 8, 11, ...**

➤ Write an algebraic expression.
Use a variable, such as n, to represent the
term number.
Each term increases by 3.
Substitute $n = 1, 2, 3, 4, ...$ into $3n$.

$3(1) = 3$
$3(2) = 6$
$3(3) = 9$
$3(4) = 12$

Each term value in the pattern is 1 less than $3n$.
So, the expression $3n - 1$ produces the pattern.
Substitute $n = 10$ into the expression.
$3(10) - 1 = 29$
The 10th term is 29.

1. Substitute $n = 1, 2, 3, 4, 5$, and 6 to complete the number pattern in each table. Describe each pattern. Then write a pattern rule.

a) $n + 1$

n	$n + 1$
1	2
2	3
3	
4	
5	
6	

b) $3n + 1$

n	$3n + 1$
1	4
2	7
3	
4	
5	
6	

c) $4n - 3$

n	$4n - 3$
1	
2	
3	
4	
5	
6	

a) The pattern begins with _____. To get to the next term, _____.

Pattern rule: _____

b) _____

Pattern rule: _____

c) _____

Pattern rule: _____

2. Here is a number pattern. 7, 9, 11, 13, 15, . . .

a) Describe the pattern. Write a pattern rule.

_____

_____

HINT

Look at the difference between 2 consecutive terms.

Pattern rule: _____

b) Use a table to find the 10th term. From the table, the 10th term is _____.

Term Number	1	2	3	4	5	...	10
Term Value							

c) Write an expression for the nth term. _____

d) Use the expression to find the 50th term. _____

3. Here is a number pattern. $\frac{1}{2}, \frac{1}{4}, \frac{1}{6}, \frac{1}{8}, \frac{1}{10}, \ldots$

    a) Write an expression for the nth term. _____

    b) Use the expression to find the 10th term. _____

4. Here is a number pattern. 5, 11, 17, 23, 29, $\ldots$

    a) Complete: Each term value is _____ less than _____ times the term number.

    b) Write an expression for the nth term. _____

    c) Use the expression to find the 100th term. _____

5. For this number pattern: 1, 6, 11, 16, 21, $\ldots$

    a) Write a pattern rule. _____

    b) Graph the pattern.
        Use the graph to find the 9th term.

    _____

    c) Write an expression for the nth term.

    _____

    d) Use the expression to find the 75th term.

    _____

Graph of Number Pattern

Term value (vertical axis) / *Term number* (horizontal axis)

6. Here is the beginning of a number pattern.
2, 4, $\ldots$

    a) Extend the pattern in 2 different ways.

    _____

    _____

    b) Write a pattern rule for each.

    _____

    _____

    _____

H I N T

Look for common factors between 2 consecutive terms.

    c) Write an expression for the nth term for each pattern rule. Find the 8th term of each.

_____

_____

218

Quick Review

At Home At School

➤ The perimeter, the area, or the number of shapes used to build a growing figure pattern form a number pattern. The *n*th term is called the *n*th frame.

➤ You can also use a table, a graph, or an algebraic expression to describe these growing geometric patterns.

In this pattern of growing picture frames, each frame border is made from square tiles.

 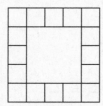 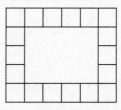 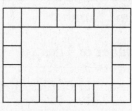

| Frame 1 | Frame 2 | Frame 3 | Frame 4 |

This table shows the number of tiles used to make each border.

Frame Number	1	2	3	4
Number of Tiles	14	16	18	20

The numbers 14, 16, 18, 20, . . . form a number pattern.

The pattern rule is: Start at 14. Add 2 each time.
The pattern can be illustrated by a graph.

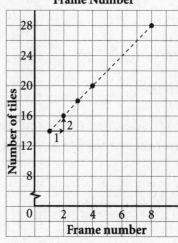

Number of Tiles against Frame Number

The graph starts at (1, 14).
To get to the next point, move 1 right and 2 up.
Moving 1 right is the increase in the frame number.
Moving 2 up is the increase in the number of tiles.

From the graph, you can find the number of tiles used to build each frame.
For the 8th frame, 28 square tiles are needed.

Each term in the number pattern increases by 2.
Adding 2 each time indicates a pattern where the term number is multiplied by 2.

The number of tiles for each frame is 12 more than 2 times the frame number.
So, an algebraic expression for the *n*th term in the pattern is: $2n + 12$

To find the number of tiles in the 100th frame, substitute $n = 100$ into the expression:
$2(100) + 12 = 212$

Practice

1. Here is a pattern of figures made with congruent square tiles.

Frame 1   Frame 2   Frame 3   Frame 4

a) Use a table to determine the number of tiles in each frame.

Frame Number	1	2	3	4
Number of Tiles	4	8		

The number of tiles in each frame is a multiple of _____.

The pattern rule is: _____

b) Graph the pattern. How does the graph illustrate the pattern?

The graph starts at _____.

To get to the next point, move

_____.

Moving _____ is the increase

in the _____.

Moving _____ is the increase

in the _____.

**Number of Tiles against
Frame Number**

c) Write an algebraic expression for the number of tiles in any frame.

_____

d) The number of tiles in the 18th frame is: _____

2. Use the pattern from question 1. The side length of each square tile is 1 unit. Complete this table for the perimeter of each frame.

Frame Number	1	2	3	4
Perimeter (units)	8	16		

a) What pattern do you see in the perimeters?

_____

_____

b) Write an algebraic expression for
the perimeter of any frame.

_____

HINT

Adding a number each
time indicates a pattern where
the term number is multiplied by
that number.

c) Find the perimeter of the 23rd frame.

_____

3. Here is a pattern of triangles made with congruent toothpicks.

Frame 1   Frame 2   Frame 3   Frame 4

a) Use this table to record the number of toothpicks in each frame.

Frame Number	1	2	3	4
Number of Toothpicks				

b) What pattern do you see?

_____

_____

c) Write an algebraic expression for the number of toothpicks in the nth frame.
Explain how you found it.

_____

_____

_____

_____

d) Find the number of toothpicks needed for Frame 32.

_____

221

Quick Review

➤ An equation is a statement that two algebraic expressions are equal.

Recall that you used coloured tiles to model integers.

　■ –1　　　□ +1

A black tile models –1.
A white tile models +1.
These two unit tiles form a zero pair.

You can also use coloured tiles to represent variables.

　□ +x

　■ –x

A white tile models +x.
A black tile models –x.
These two variable tiles form a zero pair.

Recall how you used algebra tiles to solve an equation in *Unit 1*.
To keep the balance of an equation, what you do to one side, you must also do to the other side.

For example, to solve $2x = 6 - x$, use algebra tiles to represent the equation.

Isolate the x-tiles on the left by adding 1 white x-tile to make a zero pair on the right. Then remove the zero pair.

There are 3 x-tiles. So, arrange the unit tiles into 3 equal groups.

One x-tile equals 2 white tiles. So, $x = 2$

➤ To verify the solution, substitute $x = 2$ into the equation.
Left side: $2(2) = 4$　　　　Right side: $6 - (2) = 4$
Since the left side equals the right side, $x = 2$ is correct.

1. Write an equation that can be represented by each arrangement of algebra tiles.

a) _____

b)  _____

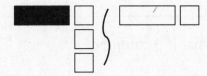

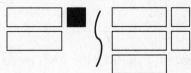

2. Use algebra tiles to solve each equation in question 1.
   Sketch the arrangements of tiles to show the steps.

a) $x =$ _____

b) $x =$ _____

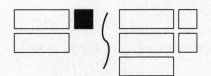

Isolate the *x*-tiles on the right side.

Add _____ *x*-tiles on the left to make zero pairs.

Isolate the unit tiles on the left side.

Add _____ unit tiles on the right to make zero pairs.

To verify the solution, substitute

$x =$ _____ into $3 - x = x + 1$.

Left side: $3 -$ _____ = _____

Right side: _____ + 1 = _____

Left side _____ right side.

Isolate the *x*-tiles on the right side.

Add _____ *x*-tiles on the left to make zero pairs.

Isolate the unit tiles on the left side.

Add _____ unit tiles on the right to make zero pairs.

To verify the solution, substitute

$x =$ _____ into $2x - 1 = 3x + 2$.

Left side: $2($_____$) - 1 =$ _____

Right side: $3($_____$) + 2 =$ _____

Left side _____ right side.

3. Interpret each equation in words.

a) $6x - 4 = 4x + 2$ _____

_____

b) $5 - 3x = 2x$ _____

_____

4. Write an algebraic equation for each word equation.
Let x represent the unknown number.

Tip

You can use different letters to represent the number.

a) Seven times a number plus three equals twelve minus two times the number.

_____

b) Double a number minus four equals triple the number plus five.

_____

5. Use algebra tiles to solve each equation in question 4. What is the number?

a) Equation: _____ b) Equation: _____

  $x =$ _____ $x =$ _____

Verify your solution.

Left side: _____   Left side: _____

Right side: _____   Right side: _____

_____   _____

_____   _____

Quick Review

➤ Recall that in *Unit 1* you solved equations algebraically.
The solutions were whole numbers.
You can use the same method to solve an equation where the solution is a negative integer, a fraction, or a decimal.
For example, to solve $3x = 6 - x$ algebraically, use inverse operations.

$$3x = 6 - x$$
$$3x + x = 6 - x + x \qquad \text{To isolate } x \text{ on the left side, add } x \text{ to each side.}$$
$$4x = 6$$
$$\frac{4x}{4} = \frac{6}{4} \qquad \text{Since you have } x \text{ multiplied by 4, divide each side by 4.}$$
$$x = \frac{3}{2}, \text{ or } 1\frac{1}{2}$$

To verify the solution, substitute $x = \frac{3}{2}$ into $3x = 6 - x$.

Left side: $3x = 3\left(\frac{3}{2}\right)$ Right side: $6 - x = 6 - \frac{3}{2}$
$$= \frac{9}{2} \qquad\qquad\qquad\qquad = \frac{12}{2} - \frac{3}{2}$$
$$\qquad\qquad\qquad\qquad\qquad\qquad = \frac{9}{2}$$

Since the left side equals the right side, $x = \frac{3}{2}$ is correct.

➤ You can use equations to solve problems related to number patterns when the nth term and its term value are known.
For example, the nth term of a pattern is $2n - 7$ and its term value is 11.
To find the term number, you solve this equation: $2n - 7 = 11$

$$2n - 7 = 11$$
$$2n - 7 + 7 = 11 + 7 \qquad \text{To isolate } n \text{ on the left side, add 7 to each side.}$$
$$2n = 18$$
$$\frac{2n}{2} = \frac{18}{2} \qquad \text{Divide each side by 2.}$$
$$n = 9$$

➤ Inspection and systematic trial are two other methods for solving equations.
You can solve $2n - 7 = 11$ by inspection:
Think: what do you subtract 7 from to get 11? You subtract 7 from 18.
Then think: what do you multiply 2 by to get 18? The answer is 9. So, $n = 9$

You can use a calculator to solve the same equation by systematic trial.
Substitute different numbers for n until the left side of the equation equals 11.

Use algebra, inspection, or systematic trial to solve an equation.

HINT

To solve an equation, what you do to one side, you must also do to the other side.

1. Solve each equation.

a) $8x - 7 = 3$ b) $5 = 3n - 6$

$8x - 7 + \underline{\hspace{2cm}} = 3 + \underline{\hspace{2cm}}$

$8x = \underline{\hspace{1.5cm}}$

$x = \underline{\hspace{1.5cm}}$ $n = \underline{\hspace{1.5cm}}$

2. Write, then solve, an equation to answer each question. Verify the solution.

a) One-half of a number added to 8 is 14. Let n be the number.

Equation: $\underline{\hspace{6cm}}$ $n = \underline{\hspace{1.5cm}}$

To verify the solution, substitute $n = \underline{\hspace{1.5cm}}$ into the equation.

Left side: Right side:

b) Fourteen less than four times a number is equal to 1 added to the number. Let y be the number.

Equation: $\underline{\hspace{6cm}}$ $y = \underline{\hspace{1.5cm}}$

To verify the solution, substitute $y = \underline{\hspace{1.5cm}}$ into the equation.

Left side: Right side:

3. The nth term of a number pattern is $3n + 7$.

    a) What is the first term?

        The term number for the first term is _____. Substitute $n =$ _____ into $3n + 7$.

        $3($_____$) + 7 =$ _____

        The first term is _____.

    b) Which term has each of these term values?

        i) 49   **ii)** 118   **iii)** 39

        The term number for the term value of 49 is _____.

        The term number for the term value of 118 is _____.

        The term number for the term value of 39 is _____.

        Are your answers reasonable? Explain.

        _____

        _____

        _____

4. Kiren has 45 autographs of celebrities in his collection.
Each week he aims at getting 4 more by shopping on the Internet.
If he is successful every week, how long will it take him to get a total of 113 autographs?

Tip
Remember to verify your solution.

    It will take Kiren _____ weeks to get 113 autographs in his collection.

In Your Words

Here are some of the important mathematical words of this unit.
Build your own glossary by recording definitions and examples here. The first one is done for you.

algebraic expression _a_
mathematical statement containing a
variable. It may include numbers and
operations
For example, 3x − 1

variable

equation

distributive property

expand

pattern rule

List other mathematical words you need to know.

Unit Review

LESSON

10.1 **1.** Use the distributive property of multiplication to expand.

a) $7(h + 3)$ b) $8(10 + 5n)$ c) $9(4x + 6y + 2)$

= _____   = _____   = _____

= _____   = _____   = _____

10.2 **2.** Here is a number pattern. 3, 7, 11, 15, 19, . . .

a) Describe the pattern. Write a pattern rule.

_____

Pattern rule: _____

b) Use a table to find the 10th term. From the table, the 10th term is _____.

Term Number	1	2	3	4	5	...	10
Term Value							

c) Write an expression for the nth term.

_____

d) Use the expression to find the 85th term.

_____

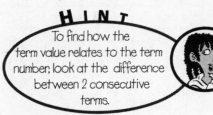

HINT

To find how the term value relates to the term number, look at the difference between 2 consecutive terms.

10.3 **3.** Here is a pattern made from congruent square tiles.

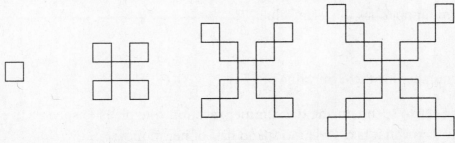

Frame 1   Frame 2   Frame 3   Frame 4

a) Use a table to determine the number of tiles in each frame.

Frame Number	1	2	3	4
Number of Tiles				

229

What pattern do you see in the table?

The number of tiles in each frame is _____.

The pattern rule is: _____

b) Graph the pattern.

c) Write an algebraic expression for the number of tiles in any frame.

d) The number of tiles in the 25th frame is:

_____

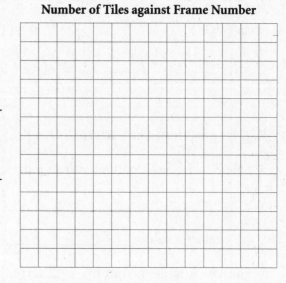

Number of Tiles against Frame Number

4. Interpret each equation in words.
Use algebra tiles to solve the equation.

10.4

a) $4 = 9 - 5x$

b) $5x + 4 = 2x - 5$

_____

_____

_____

_____

_____

_____

$x = $ _____

$x = $ _____

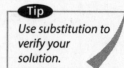

Tip
Use substitution to verify your solution.

10.5 **5.** The nth term of a number pattern is $4n + 5$.
Which term number has the term value 77?

The term number for the term value of 77 is _____.

6. Helen has $480 to spend during the summer vacation. She plans to spend $16 per day. How many days will it take Helen to spend half of her money?

Helen will spend half of the money in _____ days.

Probability

Just for Fun

Dartboard Design

The diagram shows a dartboard design drawn
on 0.5-cm grid paper.
The side length of each square is 1 unit.

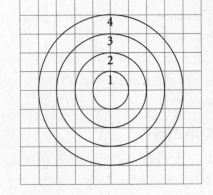

Use the formula for finding the area of a circle:
$A = \pi r^2$, where r is the radius of the circle
Find the area of each region on the dartboard.
Leave π in your answers.

Region 1: _____ units^2

Region 2: _____ units^2

Region 3: _____ units^2

Region 4: _____ units^2

Do the 4 areas form a number pattern? If so, write a pattern rule.

_____

Determine the probabilities that a dart thrown at random will land on the 4 regions.

Region 1: _____   Region 2: _____

Region 3: _____   Region 4: _____

A 5th concentric circle with radius 5 units is added to the design.

Use your pattern rule to find the area of the 5th region. _____ units^2

Find the new probabilities that a dart thrown at random will land on the 5 regions.

_____

_____

Experimental Probability

The **experimental probability** of an event occurring is: $\dfrac{\text{Number of times the event occurs}}{\text{Total number of trials}}$

This value may be written as a fraction, decimal, or percent.

Another name for experimental probability is **relative frequency**.

Example 1

In baseball, a batting average is a relative frequency of the number of hits.
The number of times a player goes to bat is the player's "at bats".

This table shows data for 3 players on a
baseball team.
Calculate the batting average of each player.
Write your answer as a fraction and as a
decimal.

Name	At Bats	Hits
Brenna	35	17
Andy	32	13
Yuki	29	9

Tip

A batting average is always written with 3 decimal places.

Solution

To calculate each player's batting average,
divide the number of hits by the number of at bats.

Brenna: $\dfrac{17}{35} \doteq 0.486$ Andy: $\dfrac{13}{32} \doteq 0.406$ Yuki: $\dfrac{9}{29} \doteq 0.310$

✔ Check

1. a) A quality-control inspector tested 415 computer screens and found 19 defective.
   What is the relative frequency of finding a defective computer screen?

   Relative frequency $= \dfrac{\text{Number of defective computer screens found}}{\text{Total number of tests}} = \underline{\quad} \doteq \underline{\qquad}$

   b) A charitable organization uses telemarketing to get donations of used clothing.
   For every 40 phone calls made, on average, 32 donations are made.
   What is the probability of getting a donation over the phone?

   Experimental probability $= \dfrac{}{\text{Total number of phone calls made}}$

   $= \dfrac{}{}$

   $= \underline{\qquad}$ or $\underline{\qquad}$%

Theoretical Probability

When the outcomes are equally likely, the **theoretical probability**, or simply, probability of an event is: $\frac{\text{Number of favourable outcomes}}{\text{Number of possible outcomes}}$

You can use theoretical probability to predict how many times a particular event will occur when an experiment is repeated many times.

Example 2

Alessio shuffles a set of cards labelled 1 to 5 and places them face down. Then he picks a card.

a) What is the probability of getting a number greater than 3 on the card?

b) Suppose Alessio repeats this experiment 20 times. Predict how many times a number greater than 3 will show.

Solution

When a card is picked, there are 5 possible outcomes: 1, 2, 3, 4, 5
The outcomes are equally likely.

a) A number greater than 3 is 4 or 5. So, there are 2 favourable outcomes.
The probability of getting a number greater than 3 on the card is: $\frac{2}{5}$

b) The predicted number of times a number greater than 3 will show is:
$\frac{2}{5} \times 20 = 8$

2. A number cube labelled 1 to 6 is rolled. The outcomes are equally likely.

a) What is the probability of rolling a number greater than 2?

A number greater than 2 is: _____

Probability = $\dfrac{\rule{3cm}{0.4pt}}{\text{Number of possible outcomes}}$ = _____ = _____

b) What is the probability of rolling a 1 or 2?

_____

c) The number cube is rolled 45 times. Predict how many times a 1 or 2 will show.

_____

Quick Review

➤ The formula for theoretical probability is: Probability $= \frac{\text{Number of favourable outcomes}}{\text{Number of possible outcomes}}$

When *all* the outcomes of an event are favourable, the numerator and denominator are equal, and the probability is 1.

When *no* outcomes of an event are favourable, the numerator equals 0, and the probability is 0.

➤ You can use a scale from 0 to 1 to mark the probability of an event.
For an impossible event, the probability that it will occur is 0, or 0%.
For a certain event, the probability that it will occur is 1, or 100%.

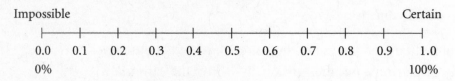

➤ A box contains 6 music CDs and 10 movie CDs.
You pick a CD from the box without looking.

Number of possible outcomes is: 6 + 10 = 16

The probability of picking a music CD is: $\frac{6}{16} = \frac{3}{8}$
The probability of picking a movie CD is: $\frac{10}{16} = \frac{5}{8}$
The probability of picking a music or movie CD is: $\frac{3}{8} + \frac{5}{8} = 1$

This last event is certain to occur.
The probability of picking an educational CD is 0.
This event is impossible.

➤ Events such as "raining today" and "not raining today" are complementary events.
Complementary events have probabilities adding up to 1.

For example, if the chance (probability) of raining today is 20%,
the chance of not raining today will be: 100% − 20% = 80%

In the case of the box containing only 6 music CDs and 10 movie CDs,
the events of picking a music CD and picking a movie CD are complementary.
When a music CD is not picked, the CD picked will be a movie CD.

1. Place the letter of each event on this number line at the value that best matches the probability of the event.

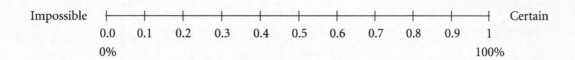

Impossible
0.0 0.1 0.2 0.3 0.4 0.5 0.6 0.7 0.8 0.9 1   Certain
0%   100%

A Without looking, Julia picks a green ball from of a bowl of identical balls with 7 red balls, 5 yellow balls, and 4 green balls.

B Thursday immediately follows Friday.

C Roll a 1, 3, or 6 on a number cube labelled 1 to 6.

D On one single spin, the pointer on this spinner lands on a shaded region.

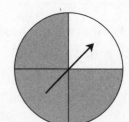

E There is a 40% chance of rain today.

F There is no snow in Ontario in July.

2. **a)** A survey indicates that 35% of voters will vote for a certain political party in the next municipal election. What is the probability that a voter will not vote for the political party in the next election?

_____

b) Suppose there are 253 681 voters. Predict:

i) how many voters will vote for the political party

HINT

Multiply the probability by the total number of voters.

_____ voters will vote for the political party.

ii) how many will not vote for the political party

Key to success

To solve a problem that involves a prediction, always check the reasonableness of your answer by estimation. If needed, round large numbers and use mental math to come up with a quick estimate.

_____ voters will not vote for the political party.

3. Two number cubes, each labelled 1 to 6, are rolled.
This table shows the possible sums showing on the number cubes.

a) Which sum is the most likely to show?
Justify your answer.

_____

_____

_____

_____

_____

_____

		First Cube					
		1	**2**	**3**	**4**	**5**	**6**
Second Cube	**1**	2	3	4	5	6	7
	2	3	4	5	6	7	8
	3	4	5	6	7	8	9
	4	5	6	7	8	9	10
	5	6	7	8	9	10	11
	6	7	8	9	10	11	12

Tip
Which sum
appears most
often? least
often?

b) Which sums are the least likely to show?
Justify your answer.

_____

_____

_____

c) Name a sum that is impossible. Explain.

_____

_____

d) Describe a certain event for this experiment. Explain.

_____

_____

e) Which sums have an equal probability of showing?
Express each probability as a fraction, a decimal, and a percent.
Round to 3 decimal places or to the tenth of a percent if necessary.

Quick Review

➤ When the outcomes of an experiment are equally likely, you can use a tree diagram to find the probability of a particular outcome.

In the *Spin-Sum* game, each of the 2 players spins a spinner in this diagram once.

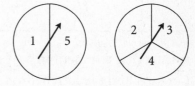

If the sum of their spins is an even number, Player A gets 1 point.

If the sum of their spins is an odd number, Player B gets 1 point.

This tree diagram lists all the possible sums.

There are 6 possible outcomes.

First Spin	Second Spin	Sum

Two outcomes are even: 4, 8
Probability of an even sum is:
$\frac{2}{6} = \frac{1}{3} \doteq 0.33$, or about 33%

Four outcomes are odd: 3, 5, 7, 9
Probability of an odd sum is:
$\frac{4}{6} = \frac{2}{3} \doteq 0.67$, or about 67%

```
First Spin    Second Spin    Sum
                    2          3
           1 <      3          4
                    4          5
Start <
                    2          7
           5 <      3          8
                    4          9
```

➤ The *Spin-Sum* game is not a fair game because Player A can score only 2 out of 6 points while Player B can score 4 out of 6 points.

A game is fair when the players have an equal chance of winning.

To make the game fair: Player A scores 1 point if the sum of their spins is less than 6.
Player B scores 1 point if the sum of their spins is greater than 6.
Then each player will have an equal chance of winning.

➤ Two players played the *Spin-Sum* game 50 times.
There were 26 sums less than 6 and 24 sums greater than 6.
The experimental probability of a sum less than 6 is: $\frac{26}{50} = 0.52$, or 52%
The experimental probability of a sum greater than 6 is $\frac{24}{50} = 0.48$, or 48%
These experimental probabilities differ from the theoretical probabilities of 50% each.

The greater the number of times the game is played, the closer the theoretical and experimental probabilities may be.

1. What is another way to make the *Spin-Sum* game fair? Justify your answer.

Tip

Look for prime numbers in the possible outcomes.

_____

_____

_____

_____

2. The four faces of a tetrahedron are labelled 1 to 4.
A coin is tossed and the tetrahedron is rolled.
For the tetrahedron, the number on the face that lands is noted.
Complete this tree diagram to list the possible outcomes.

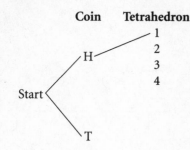

Coin	Tetrahedron	Outcome
	1	H1
H	2	
	3	
	4	
Start		
T		

Write the theoretical probability of each.

a) a head and a 4 _____

b) a tail and an even number

_____

c) a head or tail and an odd number

_____

3. Fran and Aidan each designs a way to play the *Product 24* game.

Fran designs a spinner with 4 equal sectors
labelled with the numbers 3, 4, 6, and 8.
The pointer on the spinner is spun twice.
To win this spinner game, a player must spin
2 numbers whose product is 24.

Fran's Spinner

Aidan designs a set of 4 cards labelled with the
numbers 2, 3, 8, and 12.
The cards are placed face down.
One card is selected at random and replaced.
Then a second card is selected at random.
To win this card game, a player must select
2 cards with numbers whose product is 24.

Aidan's Cards

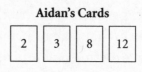

a) Complete this tree diagram for Fran's *Product 24* game.

HINT
A tree diagram can branch out vertically.

Start

First Spin   3   4   6   8

Second Spin   3   4   6   8   __ __ __ __   __ __ __ __   __ __ __ __

Product   9 __ __ __   __ __ __ __   __ __ __ __   __ __ __ __

Number of possible outcomes: _____   Number of favourable outcomes: _____

Probability of getting a product of 24 is: _____

b) Draw a tree diagram for Aidan's *Product 24* game.

Number of possible outcomes: _____   Number of favourable outcomes: _____

Probability of getting a product of 24 is: _____

c) In which game does a player have a better chance of winning?
Explain your answer.

_____

_____

Quick Review

➤ A **simulation** is a probability experiment that imitates a real-life situation. For certain events, a simulation is more practical than gathering data.

A simulation model must have the same number of outcomes as the real situation. This table shows the model to use for each number of equally likely outcomes.

Model Number of Outcomes	
coin	2
tetrahedron with 4 faces labelled 1 to 4	4
number cube labelled 1 to 6	6
spinner divided into *n* equal sectors	*n*
coin and number cube labelled 1 to 6	12
coin and spinner divided into 5 equal sectors	10

➤ To determine the probability that 3 out of 5 Grade 8 students were born on the same day of the week, Monday for example, you can use this simulation.
Design a spinner with 7 congruent sectors, one for each day of the week.

Spin the spinner 5 times, once for each of 5 students.
Conduct the experiment 100 times.
Record the number of times Monday occurred
exactly 3 times out of the 5 spins.

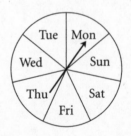

An estimate of the probability is:
$$\frac{\text{Number of times Monday occurred 3 times out of 5 spins}}{100}$$
The more often a simulation experiment is repeated, the more accurate the estimate.

Practice

1. Write the number of equally likely outcomes that can be simulated using each model.

   a) a coin and a spinner divided into 3 equal sectors _____ × _____ = _____

   b) a coin and a tetrahedron with faces labelled 1 to 4 _____

   c) 2 number cubes, each labelled 1 to 6 _____

2. In a Grade 8 class, for a group of 8 students, what is the probability that more than half of the students will have birthdays the same month?

Tip
Think: What does more than half mean?

   a) What simulation model could you use? Explain.

   _____

   _____

   b) List the possible outcomes and what they represent.

   _____

   _____

   _____

   c) Describe the simulation.

   _____

   _____

   d) The experiment is conducted 100 times. An estimate of the probability is:

   _____

3. The weather forecast for each of the next 4 days is a 50% chance of snow.

   a) What could you use to simulate a chance of 50%? Explain.

   _____

   _____

   b) Describe a simulation to estimate the probability that it will snow all 4 days.

   _____

   _____

   _____

   c) The simulation described in part b is conducted. What is the estimated probability?

   _____

d) Draw a tree diagram to calculate the probability of getting snow all 4 days.

Tip

Review Lesson 11.2 for skills in drawing tree diagrams.

Number of possible outcomes: _____   Number of favourable outcomes: _____

Probability of getting snow all 4 days is: _____

4. a) How could you use the method in question 3 to estimate the probability that in a family of 4 children, 2 or more are boys? Explain.

_____

_____

_____

_____

_____

b) Use the tree diagram in question 3 to calculate the probability that in a family of 4 children, 2 or more are boys. Show your work.

Quick Review

Odds refers to the likelihood of an event occurring.
In sports, the likelihood of a team winning or losing is described in terms of odds.

➤ The **odds in favour** of an event are described as the number of favourable outcomes
to the number of unfavourable outcomes.
For example, in a wallet containing 5 nickels, 4 dimes, 8 quarters, 3 loonies, and
5 toonies, a coin falls out. The odds in favour of the coin being a quarter are 8 to 17
because 8 of the coins are quarters and 17 are not.

➤ The **odds against** an event are described as the ratio of the number of unfavourable
outcomes to the number of favourable outcomes.
In the above example, the odds against the coin being a toonie are 20 to 5 because
20 coins are not toonies and 5 are.
You can divide each term by the common factor 5 to write 20 to 5 as 4 to 1.

Practice

1. A card is drawn at random from a standard deck of cards.

a) Find the odds in favour of drawing a club.

There are _____ cards in a deck. _____ cards are clubs.

So, there are _____ favourable outcomes and _____ unfavourable outcomes.

The odds in favour of drawing a club are _____.

Divide the terms by their common factor _____.

The odds in favour of drawing a club are _____.

b) What are the odds against drawing a 9?

Number of favourable outcomes: _____

Number of unfavourable outcomes: _____

HINT

Find the number of
cards that are 9s
and the number that
are not 9s.

The odds against drawing a 9 are _____.

2. What are the odds in favour of each event?

a) getting the number 4 or less when a number cube labelled 1 to 6 is rolled

_____

b) getting a 5 or a 6 when a card is randomly picked from
a deck of playing cards

Tip

Think: How many 5s or 6s are in a deck of cards?

_____

c) getting a perfect square when two number cubes labelled 1 to 6
are rolled and the numbers are multiplied

_____

3. What are the odds against each event in question 2?

a) _____   b) _____   c) _____

4. The probability that the school ringette team will win the city championship is 65%.

a) What are the odds in favour of the ringette team winning the city championship?
Show your work.

b) What are the odds against the ringette team winning the city championship?

_____

5. a) Describe an event of which the odds in favour are 2 to 3. Explain.

_____

_____

Tip

Use an example that describes weather.

_____

b) What are the odds against the event? _____

In Your Words

Here are some of the important mathematical words of this unit.
Build your own glossary by recording definitions and examples here. The first one is done for you.

experimental probability _also called relative frequency; an estimated probability calculated from experimental results_

The formula is: $\dfrac{\text{Number of times the event occurs}}{\text{Total number of trials}}$

theoretical probability _____

simulation _____

complementary events _____

probability range _____

odds _____

List other mathematical words you need to know.

_____

Unit Review

11.1 **1.** Find the probability of each event. Place the letter of each event on this number line
at the value that best matches the probability of the event.

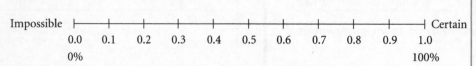

> **Tip**
>
> *Probability equals
> the number of
> favourable
> outcomes divided
> by the number of
> possible
> outcomes.*

A Without looking, Steve picks a purple marker from a can containing

4 black markers, 9 purple markers, and 2 yellow markers. _____

B There are 7 days in a week. _____

C There are 29 days in February. _____

D The complementary event of C. _____

E A coin is tossed twice and lands with 1 head and 1 tail. _____

F Summer immediately follows winter. _____

2. Larry conducted a survey and found that 45% of the 129 Grade 8 students at his
school studied 30 min or less for their math test.
How many students studied more than 30 min? Explain your answer.

_____ students studied more than 30 min for the math test.

11.2 **3.** In a board game, the players spin the
pointers on both spinners.

The number on Spinner 1 is divided
by the number on Spinner 2 to give
the Quotient.

The player moves that number of
squares on the game board.

Spinner 1

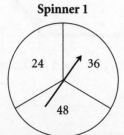

Spinner 2

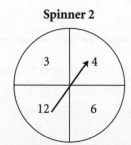

a) Complete this tree diagram for the possible quotients.

Spinner 1	Spinner 2	Quotient
	3	8

24

Start

b) What is the probability of getting a quotient that is a perfect square?

List the quotients in the tree diagram that are perfect squares: _____

Number of possible outcomes: _____   Number of favourable outcomes: _____

Probability of getting a perfect square is: _____

c) What is the probability of getting a quotient that is an even number?

Number of possible outcomes: _____   Number of favourable outcomes: _____

Probability of getting an even number is: _____

d) What is the probability of getting a quotient that is a multiple of 4?

Number of possible outcomes: _____   Number of favourable outcomes: _____

Probability of getting a multiple of 4 is: _____

11.3 **4.** A multiple-choice test has 10 questions. Each question has 4 answer choices.
To pass the test, a student must score 5 correct answers.
A student randomly chooses an answer for each question.

a) What simulation model could you use to estimate the probability that the student will pass the test? Explain.

_____

_____

b) Design a simulation to find out. Explain.

_____

_____

_____

_____

_____

11.4 5. A card is drawn at random from a standard deck of cards.

Tip
To simplify the odds, divide the terms by their common factor.

  a) What are the odds in favour of drawing a heart?

    There are _____ cards in a deck. _____ cards are hearts.

    So, there are _____ favourable outcomes and _____ unfavourable outcomes.

    The odds in favour of drawing a heart are _____.

  b) What are the odds against drawing a 4 or 5? Show your work.

    The odds against drawing a 4 or 5 are _____.

6. What are the odds in favour of each event? Explain.

  a) getting 2 heads when a coin is tossed twice

  b) getting a prime number when a card is randomly picked from a deck of cards

7. The odds against a school team winning the city championship are 7 to 8. Does the team have a good chance of winning? Justify your answer.

248